C000002367

LEAVES FROM A VICTORIAN DIARY

LEAVES FROM A VICTORIAN DIARY

❧❧
❧❧

by
Edward Leeves

With an Introduction by
John Sparrow

An Alison Press Book
Secker & Warburg · London

First Published in England 1985 by
The Alison Press/Secker & Warburg Limited
54 Poland Street, London W1V 3DF

Introduction Copyright © 1985 by John Sparrow

British Library Cataloguing in Publication Data

Leeves, Edward

   Leaves from a Victorian diary.

   1. Leeves, Edward   2. Great Britain—Biography
   I. Title
   941.081'092'4   CT788.L42/

   ISBN 0–436–24370–9

Printed and bound in Great Britain by
Mackays of Chatham Ltd

Contents

Introduction   xi

Leaves From A Victorian Diary   1

Appendix: The Diarist's Will   120

Epilogue   125

become indifferent to everything — for such is the case. I have no pleasure in anything, & my only desire is to close this unprofitable existence, for life it cannot be called, as soon as possible. My poor Boy was the only interest I had made for myself, & he was taken away! What might have happened had he lived it is now vain to dream of; but he has left nothing behind, & be his loss for good or for evil, I am now all alone in this weary world. For the last ten days, since I came from Leamington, save calling on Mr Scott for a quarter of an hour, I have not seen a face I knew, & this in London. On looking back to kill the time this snowy day, I find that, like true human nature I grieve but little of those few days since I came to England in which I was really happy. I too confidently hoped that they were only the introduction to many, many of the same, or even happier; and now that they are gone never to return, I wonder that I should have noticed them so little. What wd I now give for one hour of them each again. There was so much that I had to say, & to ask; so much to be done & arranged! All had been delayed, for an absence of three weeks was as nothing in our calculations.

13. Same bitter cold. This day five Calendar months we went to Gravesend: nineteen weeks since He went down to the Home Grounds for the last time! In spite of the cold I cd not stay at home, & I went on the Knightsbridge road to where we parked for ever — Then to Bn Church yard, & knelt on his frozen grave & prayed for mercy for him & that I might soon sleep as he does, & kissed the name on the cold stone which marks the last abode of "The young, the kind, the beautiful, the brave." I have been pondering on which side the advantage is, whether to have relations & friends to sorrow,

one was fondly attached, or to be as I am almost alone. If I had the courage to put an end to an existence without charms, I should say that, decidedly, it was better to be alone. Then there would only be the leaf to take, and to go unregretting & unregretted. Even as it is with me – i.e. without that courage – I think I have the advantage. If I have nothing to love, I have nothing to consider & am, therefore, freer to act. Would all these thoughts were ended, & that I were in my Grave. To say I am quite beat down; & long to be at rest; for here it is a wearisome daily repetition of sad recollections & nothing to hope for.

The Inscription on poor Jack's tombstone runs thus
" To the Memory of

John Brand

of the Royal Horse Guards Blues

who died of Cholera

5ᵗʰ Septʳ 1849

aged 22.

Implora Pace "

14. Cloudy & the frost one of the most severe known for a long time. It seemed to take fresh force with the new Moon yesterday. Paxton is the name of the man who has got poor Jack's Horse!

15. Some cloudy atmosphere, but the frost increases in Intervals, the cold is almost insupportable; yet I certainly suffer less in Body than I have done at Venice. At any rate here are no Chilblains. My mind on the other hand sinks daily under the chilling Influence. Five kalendar

reproduced on pages 45, 46–47

Introduction

Introduction

I think I can best introduce Edward Leeves and his diary by explaining how the manuscript of its text, now printed for the first time, came into my possession, and recording the few facts that I have been able to discover concerning the diarist himself.

First, I must present to the reader Victor Cunard, the friend who placed the diary in my hands. Victor Cunard, like Edward Leeves, was an Inglese Venezianato. Born in 1898, the third son of Sir Gordon Cunard, fourth baronet, he left Eton in 1916 to join the Coldstream Guards, in which he served until the end of the War; he was Correspondent of *The Times* in Rome, 1922–7, and Assistant Correspondent in Paris, 1927–33; he served in the Political Intelligence Department of the Foreign Office during the Second World War, and died, unmarried, on 28 August 1960, in Venice, where he spent most of his time during the closing years of his life, occupying an apartment in the Palazzo Foscarini ai Carmini.

The manuscript was given to Victor – I should think in the 1940s or the early 1950s – by a neighbour in Venice, an English lady with whom he was slightly acquainted,[1] whose husband had recently died. Going through his effects, she had come upon a

[1] So far as I can remember, Victor never told me her name.

little book in a limp black binding, containing 56
leaves which carried a diary, closely written on both
sides of each leaf, covering the period 6 April 1849
to 31 July 1850. She had no idea how the book had
come into her husband's possession, and she had not
attempted to examine its contents: but she thought
it might be of interest, and, rather than destroy it,
she gladly made a present of it to her neighbour.
Victor accepted the gift, took the book home, and
glanced idly through its pages. He soon found himself fascinated by the personality of the writer and by
the story that he had to tell. He lost no time in having
a typed copy made, on which he inscribed the
appropriate title 'Leaves from a Victorian Diary',
and which he used to show to friends who he thought
might appreciate it. Not long before he died, Victor
placed the original and the typed copy in my hands,
with a view to my preparing a text for possible publication. Sir Edward Cunard, writing to me soon after
Victor's death, said that he was fulfilling his brother's
intention by making me a present of the manuscript. I am now, belatedly, giving effect to what I
believe would have been my friend's wishes by
publishing the text of this remarkable document.

Of Edward Leeves, his origins and his life-history,
I have been able to discover practically nothing
beyond what he lets fall about himself in this volume
of his diaries[1] and the few particulars that can be
gathered from his will.[2]

[1] It seems plain that Leeves was a life-long diarist, and that there
must have existed a series of his diaries, of which this is the only
volume that has survived. Perhaps Leeves himself destroyed the
rest of them in later years – cf. the entry for 6 June 1850: 'I have
been reading over, in order to destroy, old pocket books &
journals. Alas! what scenes of other days they called up!'
[2] Dated 9 July 1870. Printed as an Appendix, p. 120.

In his will, Leeves describes himself as 'formerly of Tortington in the County of Sussex, but now and for many years past residing in Venice'. An account of the Leeveses of Tortington is contained in a volume of family papers printed for private circulation in 1873.[1] The principal figure there commemorated is William Leeves (1748–1828), who for the last forty years of his life was Rector of Wrington in Somerset, and was remembered as the composer of the air 'Auld Robin Gray'. No particulars are given of Edward Leeves, who evidently cut himself off from family ties and settled in Venice at an early age. The only member of his family that Edward mentions in the surviving volume of his diaries is a deceased sister.[2]

Leeves was evidently a man of ample means who moved in good society in Venice and in London. His diary offers tempting material for the social historian, and the surviving volume perhaps deserves to be presented in a fully annotated edition, in which the friends and acquaintances who figure in its pages are identified and the allusions to contemporary events explained. But such a presentation of the material would, I think, overlay the portrait that Leeves unconsciously gives us of himself, and it is this self-portrait that makes his diary a unique and fascinating document.

[1] *In Memoriam The Rev. W. Leeves, Author of the air of 'Auld Robin Gray'. With a few notices of other members of his family.* The compiler of this volume was Mrs. Anne Moon, a great-niece of the composer of the well-known air. A genealogy of the Leeves family of Tortington is preserved in the West Sussex Records Office.

[2] 'Letters I have none to expect now that my Sister is gone' (21 May 1849). He makes no mention of contact with any member of his family during the visit to England recorded in this volume of his diary.

Of his early life this surviving volume of Leeves's diary reveals almost nothing. He must have been born in the closing years of the eighteenth century – 'one should ask for no more after 60', he says, a few days before his birthday on 5 July 1850. He provides no reminiscences of his family, his childhood, or his school-days; he did not go to Oxford or to Cambridge, and it seems that he settled in Venice when he was still a young man. There he maintained a comfortable establishment,[1] looked after by a couple – Antonio and Teresa – a man-servant, and a cook.[2] On 15 June 1849, *en route* for England, he notes in his diary that he had passed the last two years with 'never a night out of Venice'. Spending the first night of his journey at Trieste, he finds that 'the heat and confusion perfectly bewilder me'; as for Vienna, which he reached a few days later, 'its climate and the noise of the carriages drives me wild . . . The quiet of Venice covers a multitude of sins.'

In Venice he enjoyed the company of English and Italian friends. His diary gives a vivid picture of his social life: 'Went to Lady Sorell's for half an hour' (9 April 1849); 'Messrs. Dawkins, O'Conor &c. dined with me . . . Dinner detestable, tho' I had Zichy's Chef' (15 May 1849); 'Called on Mrs. O'Conor and on Contessa Balbi' (5 July 1850); 'At night I was met at the Lido by the O'Conors . . . we supped by the light of the moon on the Laguna . . . We had Ice & Champagne &c. & there were

[1] Rented from Il Conte Zen. The diary bears, inside its front cover, the address '2180 rosso Palazzo Molin'.
[2] In his will, dated twenty years later (9 May 1870), Leeves mentions 'my two women servants', and names two men-servants and a (male) cook; to all of these he bequeathed legacies.

Nicoletto Michiel and young Dolfin, &c. & it was really agreeable' (25 July 1850).

Upon this small and civilized community there descended, in the early summer of 1849, the threat of an Austrian military invasion. Leeves was in a quandary. Should he stay, and face the perils of war and the possibility of an enemy occupation? Or should he abandon his home and his possessions – 'my prints and books and pictures and reminiscences' – and take refuge in his native land? After some hesitation, he accepted the offer of a passage to Trieste in a British vessel, and went on board in the early hours of the morning of 9 June.

From Trieste he set out by rail for Berlin, stopping for a couple of nights on the way at Vienna – 'very tired & weary & disgusted at travelling without a Servant'. While in Vienna he 'went for sights' to the Belvedere and Esterhazy Galleries and made contact with one or two English acquaintances. In Berlin he spent a week (June 21–27), staying at the Hôtel du Nord: 'very fair & people civil; but much inferior in all ways to the Archduke Charles at Vienna'. As for the Belle Vue at Deutz, where he spent the next two nights, *en route* for Ostend, it was 'dear, dirty, uncivil & detestable'.

On 1 July Leeves landed at Dover. He went up to London, took lodgings in Mayfair, and renewed his contacts with his English friends and acquaintances. His diary mentions Lord and Lady Ponsonby, Lady E. Reynell ('who was very gracious'), his particular friends the Huskissons of Coolhurst in Sussex, and Lord and Lady Queensberry, whom he visited, in the course of the summer, both at Leamington and at their Scottish seat at Kinmount in Dumfriesshire.

Within a week of his arrival in England, a new element entered Leeves's life – an emotional pre-occupation that held him in thrall for the rest of the period covered by this volume of his diary: a passionate attachment to the person – and, after his death, to the memory – of Jack Brand, a trooper in the Royal Horse Guards, the 'Blues'.

The diary provides tantalizing glimpses of the progress of the affair. It was on 8 July 1849 that Leeves first set eyes on Jack Brand; he first spoke to him next day. On 10 July he left London on a visit to the Huskissons at Coolhurst. The visit lasted three weeks, during which period several letters passed between the two new friends, and they agreed to meet on the day when Leeves got back to London. For that day, 30 July, the diary records: 'Saw J.B. We went up to Albany St.' During the next fortnight, it seems, there were at least four meetings between them, including a 'Water Excursion' on the Thames on 13 August, which was repeated on the following day. Then, on 16 August, Leeves travelled north, to stay with his friends Lord and Lady Queensberry at Kinmount. He said goodbye to Jack on the previous day: 'Took leave at Kensington. Soon to meet again, I hoped.'

Leeves spent nearly three weeks at Kinmount, returning to London on 4 September, in time to keep a rendezvous with Jack on the following day. The entry in the diary for 4 September breaks off at the end of a page with the words 'To London, where', after which a number of pages have been torn out; the next surviving entry is for 16 December.

The remaining pages of Leeves's diary explain this hiatus in the record. Leeves evidently kept the rendezvous, and waited in vain for his friend. One can imagine the fears and the suspicions that passed through his mind.

Inquiries at Wellington Barracks, no doubt, revealed the tragic truth. During the summer an epidemic of cholera had ravaged Europe: *The Times* of 17 December[1] recorded, retrospectively, that 'In Paris the most fatal month of Cholera was June, when 5,769 perished. In London the most fatal month was September, when 6,644 fell victims.' Jack Brand was one of the first of these many victims, dying on the very day of his appointed rendezvous with his new-found friend.

How comes it that this is the only volume of Leeves's diaries that has survived? In it he records, under the date of 6 June 1850, his wholesale destruction of 'a long series of letters, notes & recollections'; 'the next thing to be done', he goes on to say, 'is the same with my journals, & yet I go on keeping this!' It seems likely that during the twenty years he had still to live he continued to keep a diary, and he may have repeated – perhaps more than once – this annihilation of the surviving records of his personal life. If this was so, why was it that this volume of his diaries – and, it seems, this volume only – escaped destruction?

May it not be that it was because this volume recorded what was for him the most precious emotional experience of his life – so precious that he could not bring himself to destroy the record?

Paradoxically, the record is itself imperfect: several entries are deleted, and (as I have said) a number of pages – covering a period of just over three months after the tragic date, 4 September – have been

[1] Quoted by Leeves in his diary under that date.

torn out. One must, I think, conclude that, though Leeves preserved this volume, he could not bear to re-read – and perhaps did not wish others to set eyes upon – the passages in which he gave vent to his grief when it was at its most poignant.

No attempt has been made to standardize Edward Leeves's punctuation or use of capital letters, nor have his occasional spelling mistakes or wrong dates been corrected. So far as it is possible to decipher his handwriting, this version is exactly as the diarist wrote it.

John Sparrow

Diary

1849 Venice

April 6

Fine but the air is chilly, & my Mignonette with[t] scent. A new Vol. of my Diary begun! Under strange circumstances. *How* will this tragi-comedy end? and *when*? this interests me the most nearly.

7

Do.

8

Cold & cloudy. I begin to hope that the French will really not interfere. At mid-day it set in wet. The Blockade has commenced. They say the Austrians have 36 vessels under a Danish Adm[l]. The Sards gone! What next – and when? Many people, some of them Venetians – my Landlord* for instance – sent away.

9

Cloudy & showery: at night very hard rain. I went

---

* Il Conte Zen – He made his escape with[t] a Passport! much to the annoyance of the, so called, Govt.

to L^y Sorell's for half an hour, as she & Mrs. C. go to Trieste tomorrow.

10

Cold & wet. No post ag^n today, & God knows when any will arrive. I never got out, & have not suffered more from cold all the winter.

11

Weather doubtful. This cursed revolution at Genoa stops our post and we have no letters or papers for the last 4 days. My fingers are still swollen & painful, I conclude the remains of the chilblains: but they are hideous to see, & very disagreeable. It is wearisome being cut off from all communication with the rest of the world! Much rain.

12

Cold & showery. Still no french Post. M. Serruz dined with me.

13

Wet. Had a regular blow up with Favenza, who has behaved most abominably.

14

Cold & wet. Another interview with Favenza, with whom I never will have any further Intercourse, when this Job is finished. The Sard^n fleet gone, & the People very low. Would to God it were all over! I am weary past bearing of a year of such sport. No post for 10 days past.

15

Weather detestable – wet & bitterly cold, so that without a fire, which I cannot afford myself, in face of a Blockade, I am starved & frozen.

16

Uncertain & cold. Genoa surrend[d], Florence recalled the Grand Duke: here obstinacy & lies. Manin ill, but sent a lying message to the people, who insisted on news. Letters given out, but no french Papers or English, & no letters for me. Cha[s] has not written since the 8th March – a tedious time, & I have no other to hope for!

17

Bitter cold, which makes me feel very unwell. No letters or Papers still! When will this end?

18

Cold & stormy, & I unwell. At last some papers & a letter, the former to the 7th inclusive, but 3 wanting.

19

Unwell. Same inclement weather, & a violent storm at night.

20

Same weather.

21

Do. I have returned to my fires, in spite of the price of wood. The cold was quite insupportable.

22

Fine, but very cold.

23

Cold & cloudy. Time wears on apace, & we seem no nearer the End: & I yearn to get to England in June.

24

Milder with the new moon.

25

S. Marco. On Saturday I rec^d my Box from Alessandro Torlonia. A Print from a likeness by Morani, & which has a very strong & pleasing resemblance to my excellent Carlo! Alas! not for Him but for Aless° & the Princess; & all his friends! They will never see his like again in Italy! The French at Civita Vecchia. I hope this will put an end to all these tragicomedies. A fine day, but I am dull.

26

Fine. I really yearn to get to England in June, & each day leaves me disappointed that the finale seems no nearer. M. Serruz dined with me.

27

Summer seems come, & the swallows.

28

Very fine. Sicily seems to have yielded *unconditionally*! Good God! These People are worse than Madmen; they are fools!

29

Very fine.

30

Do.

May 1

Mild & springlike. They go on cannonading every night, & all night, & I get no rest. Will it ever end? At night to Mr. Mudie's.

2

Fine & pleasant, but with light clouds and showers.

3

Same. I see no signs of things coming to a close, & despair of my English journey. Nor do I understand how matters can ever be adjusted without a war. Thunder, lightening & hail, but the air mild. Messrs. O'Conor, Grignon & Mudie dined.

4

Same weather. A heavy cannonade all day from Malghera: but why, or with what result, no one knows.

5

Cloudy & threatening. My cough very troublesome. The wretches at Rome seem resolved to oppose force to the French, & I tremble for the ruin & havoc which must ensue. They have begun to demolish, &

Garibaldi is on the Monte Mario! Alas! for the years that are passed, & their many, many recollections! I am so weary of all these confusions; & I so yearn to get to England! Days & weeks & months elapse, & there seems no hope of a road being open, without much trouble, & then I must leave everything here in uncertainty. I am bewildered, & cannot tell what to do. It rained from midday & I never got out; employing myself in the melancholy occupation of sorting old letters of those dead & divided. Oh! my happy, quiet days of Therapia! I can never live again their like!

6

Fine. Fighting at the Villa Pamfili, cannonading near the Vatican, intrenching on the Pincio!!! What times to live in!

7

Showery & dull. I am quite knocked down with all this news. Here the Austrians are pushing their approaches, & have again sent a summons; but in vain. Dined at Mr. Grignon's.

8

A very heavy cannonade all night. No news from Rome that can be depended upon: but it would seem that the french had rec^d a check, or, more probably, from fear of injuring the Eternal City, relinquished the idea of entering it by force & hostilities. However their account of what took place will tell a very different tale from that of Mazzini & Co. Fine.

9

Fine. At night to Mr. O'Conor's.

10

Uncertain. I am thoroughly out of sorts & worn out
with all this confusion, which seems to get worse &
worse everywhere. Last night I heard that poor old
de Thurm was dead: the only Gentleman I have met
with in Venice of Germans or Venetians.

11

Uncertain. There seems a pause in the operations.
But things must be coming to a close in Italy, at
least. In Germany nothing but Russian arms can put
down the demagogues, I fear. How true Ld Ponsonby's anticipations have proved – that the Peace
would endure till the fruits of it proved fatal! How
much better a war five years back!

Today I was to have dined with Mr. Dawkins, but
press of writing has obliged him to put off his party.
Our last hour is coming – almost announced – for
Haynau has advised the departure of all foreigners, &
demanded that of all ships of war by the 21st Ins^t. So
here we are in a fix – to fly & leave all my little all –
the collection of so many years – or to stay, exposed
to all the dangers of an assault, internal as well as
external. At the moment we have no ship here, the
Racer having gone to Ancona yesterday. My own
impression is to stay quiet; but I shall be guided by
what others do, & by the wishes, or rather counsels,
of the Consul General. At any rate we now are
rapidly approaching to the denouement of this fatal
Tragi-comedy. What ruin to thousands! What

misery to all Italy! Surely the Preachers & agitators of all this mischief will not be allowed to escape unscathed!

12

Showery. A meeting at the Consulate, but it was merely to state what I heard yesterday. I am almost decided to run all chances & stick by my Household Gods. If I fall there are few to mourn for me, and my things are safer when I am on the spot: besides a multitude of difficulties about money & servants, &c: &, if I went, I c^d not well go to England, & leave everything to chance. At night to Mr. Mudie's.

13

A fine morning. My confounded Cook is gone mad, I believe with political excitement; but I understand that He has a brother in San Servolo. Changed my mourning for my poor Sister: who will wear any for me? Had she lived she would have been so uneasy about me that I must have retired. Now I grow more & more disposed to run all risques.

14

Fine, but a thunder Storm in the Evening. I am more & more disposed to take my chance & stay.

15

Fine. My damned Servant gone mad again. I must bear with him till I can see my way thro' this Confusion, and then dismiss him. It is utterly impossible to allow his permanent stay. Messrs. Dawkins,

O'Conor &c. dined with me. Capt. Beddoes not returned from Ancona. Dinner detestable, tho' I had Zichy's Chef: but it was more the fault of the materials than His: Service equally bad. I make no further attempts till one can feed like Xtians.

16

Same uncertain weather, with Scirocco. I unwell, & worried almost out of my senses. P^d M. Serruz £16 – for my Pictures.

17

Same, warm but uncertain. Germany appears to be returning to the anarchy of last year; & the red republicans to be making another desperate effort there, in France, & in Italy for victory. I trust that this time the cause of *order* will be better defended, & that in the struggle *al cuchillo*, which is, & must be, the legitimate Powers will unite to crush the Hydra. This time may the influence of England, too, be exerted in the cause of all that is good, & just, & righteous! There is a rumour that at Rome the Church of S. Giovanni Laterano has been burned, & the Borghese Palace, where the precious Paintings have been consumed in the Street. The Princess will have paid dear for her national prejudices! I must hope that this news, from a private letter, is false or much exaggerated: but all is to be feared, & all that is atrocious is possible from the ruffians who have usurped Power everywhere. I am sad even to my heart's core, & envy the Happiness of my poor Carlo who was taken in time. Would I were as He was! Then to die would be a blessing.

Showery. I am perfectly beaten down, & worn out. I feel that Death is the only end to all this turmoil. I do not remember ever being so thoroughly depressed.

Fine. This morning came a note from the Consul Gen¹ offering me, by desire of Capt. Beddoes, a passage to Trieste this Evening in the *Frolic*. I expressed my very grateful thanks, but was resolved to stay where I was. So now I am in for it.

Fine. The last day allowed by Haynau: but the french will not leave without orders from Paris, & the *Racer* only goes down to Malamocco. I very unwell in the night: a heavy firing was kept up, &, it seemed to me, with larger guns than hitherto. Germany is more frantic & in greater anarchy than last year; & the Reds in france struggling for another revolution there. How will, or can, it all end?

Fine. Everything seems dead. Sometimes two or three Papers arrive, but very irregularly. Letters I have none to expect now that my Sister is gone, save from Charles. I had no idea what a gap her death would make in my existence!

Fine. Our Post, I fear, is now finally stopped: as the Austrians are said to be at Ravenna. In the meantime Haynau does nothing & our agony is prolonged. At night to Mr. Mudie's.

23

Fine. We are cut off from the rest of the world, & it is a feeling of anxiety almost insupportable.

24

Cloudy. Some extracts of Trieste Papers rec^d last night. New revolutions in Germany, & very doubtful state of things in France. If I can once get away, I will go & finish my days in our own foggy England. This is our little Queen's birthday, 30 today. What has She in store for Her! Good, I fervently hope & pray! She is cast upon fearful times for all, but mostly for Sovereigns. Will English good sense keep firm in the face of this universal dissolution of all Laws, human & divine? I am completely subdued, & my solitude begins to overpower all my power of elasticity. What a selfish nature is our human one! We are dissatisfied at the thought that, dying, there is none to regret us! Thus seeking & finding pleasure in the Pain of others, & those people whom we love dear; and for what? for a regret which makes them unhappy, and of which we can not even know the existence! Strange! Dined at the Consul General's.

25

Cloudy. The new Austrian Genl, Conte de Thun, seems to be attacking with great vigour, & the Cannonade is very severe. I went to the top of a Brewery at S^a Chiara to see it, & it was a fine spectacle.

Thunder & showers, so that I was driven in without going to the Campo di Marte to see the firing, which is very heavy this afternoon, & seems much nearer for the shock makes my windows rattle. So much the better: anything would be better than this present state of things. It would be a real pleasure to me to see a Bomb fall upon one of the Palaces. It cannot last much longer: & then! – for the Austrians are resolute to have Venice at any cost. I hope there will be no mock Humanity, but that the chiefs will be made to pay for the misery they have so wantonly, & wickedly, inflicted. Alas! for Rome. I fear the ruin has been dreadful there in all ways; but cut off as we are we know nothing certain. The last french paper was of the 10th.

27

Fine. They say that all the forts have surrendered, being no longer other than a heap of ruins: so the soldiers insisted on quitting them. What next! From Rome no certain news, but, by what can be gathered from the Tuscan Papers of latest date, which profess to give news from Rome of the 20th, nothing can be worse than the state of things. The desperate wretches who govern refusing to submit, & M. Lesseps the new french minister withdrawing! Would to God I were in England out of all this infernal villainy.

28

Fine. The forts were abandoned at sunrise yesterday morning. Nevertheless the Venetians continued a fire from their boats, &c., all night: to which the Austrians made no reply. They are occupied in reestablishing the Guns of the forts, in order to turn them upon the Town. As soon as they have done so the music will recommence, & the result must be dreadful unless the Villains here yield. It cannot now be long ere the business is decided, & then I shall have no rest till I am on my road to England. It is become an imperative necessity both for mind & body to breathe in a sure & civilized country, & such I hope ours still is, in spite of Ld Palmerston.

29

Fine. The Venetians have destroyed, or are said to to have done so, for here everything that one does not see with one's own eyes is doubtful, about 30 arches of the Bridge towards Marghera. No symptom of yielding: Manin still promises succour from France; & the people of the Canna-regio are abandoning their Houses, as the Balls arrive at the extremity of that Sestiere; consequently not far from me! I am half inclined to take refuge in My Lady's House, which is more out of the way: but I am so idle, or so indifferent, that the trouble deters me. The Papers say that the English Navy has given shelter to another batch of Traitors, the Tuscans Guerrazzi, Petrucci &c. *Evviva Ld Palmerston, ed il disonore d'Inghilterra.*

30

Fine. Went & took refuge, till the Storm blows over, with the Armenians at San Lazzaro; by the kindness of Padre Gregorio Alesson. The quiet is something delightful after the confusion of Venice. My room looks into the Quadrangle; full of Roses &c., & puts me in mind of Pentia.

Fine & very hot. I am still sleepless & dyspeptic. I think the last from having been excited with the trouble of moving. All is kindness here, impossible to be more so. At Venice the same obstinate resistance. I wish it were over, for I want to get to England sadly! In the Ev^g to Lido with M. & Me Gabriel.

June 1

Very fine & hot. The Assembly has met, & decided on resistance, & on leaving the supreme Gov^t in the Hands of Manin. Consequently it is impossible to see when this state of things will finish, or what the result can be, other than the destruction of Venice! The Austrians sent another – a fourth – flag of truce, who ret^d with an answer of defiance: now, therefore, nothing remains but force or retreat! The last impossible without dishonour & raising a new revolt through Lombardy.

2

Very hot. How well I am off here, in this tranquillity! and they are all so kind! But uncertainty & anxiety render me suffering, & I feel a want of change, such as I never experienced before. When will there be a possibility of escape!

3

Very hot. The same peaceable, quiet life, which suits me perfectly.

4

Same.

5

Same. Padre Gregorio left to go by steamer to Trieste, so that I quitted my hospitable quarters a day sooner than I had arranged. All were kind in pressing me to stay till things were finished; but this waiting for the Austrians is waiting for another year. Therefore I came back to my Home better for the change, grateful for all the kindness I met with, and almost longing to enroll myself in some such society. I am weary of this mortal coil, but more weary of the madness of the world. The fancy of shooting at the Sovereign has revived in England, it seems.

6

Intensely hot, and the mad folly of these Italians keeps up a constant irritation. Besides, now that I cannot get there, I am mad to be in England. The rail road is opened to Verona, & here am I almost within sight of it, hermetically blocked up!

7

Hot, cloudy Scirocco, very overpowering: some rain in the night, with much Lightening, cannonading as usual. *Corpus Domini*: how diff^t from that of 1847 at Rome! Alas for the Eternal City! for the Peace and Prosperity of this beautiful Country! Sacrificed to the ambition of some starving Advocates, and the mischievous & ignorant Policy of Ld Palmerston! The Vanity of Pio IX having led the way. Thrice happy they who went before the ruin came, Lady Coventry, and my best Carlo! To the last the misery of his Country would have been fatal. The poor Princess! The Wealth and Splendor of Alessandro! Oh! the Vanity of Human wishes! In the Ev^g Capt. Beddoes offered me a Passage to Trieste, where he goes in a day or two. I asked till tomorrow to decide. In the night a violent thunderstorm & cannonade as usual.

8

Resolved to accept. Mr. Dawkins sent to tell me that the *Racer* would sail at 3 in the morning of the 9th, so I have no time for reflection. Cloudy & languid. After dinner carried my trunk aboard. So now there is no retreat; & now I almost regret not to wait for the finale, & the opening of the strait road by Milan. I fear I shall have to go by Vienna, & perhaps by Berlin! an immense Bore. And now, too, they seem to think that 24 Hours will finish the whole. If so, as usual, I have made a mess; but I am so worn out with this kind of existence, & so desirous to get to England (why I know not) – that I could not refuse the first opportunity of escape from this Purgatory. Shall I ever see it again? Who can answer for four months forward in these days!

9

Went on board at 3 a.m. Soon after came Card^l Falconieri, Archb^p of Ravenna. We soon made acquaintance. He told me that the Villa Patrizi was destroyed as well as the various ones in the Borghese Gardens, & that the Villa Albani was threatened! What will become of those of Alessandro & Marino? Alas for Rome – Her glories are fled for ever! No wind, so we could not sail, & as it was at last settled that the *Pluton* should go in the afternoon, it became a doubt whether the *Racer* would go at all. So the Card^l, very reluctantly, transferred himself to that Steamer. I remained, by Capt. Beddoes' advice.

10

Dropped down to Malamocco, but could not get out. Showery yesterday & today.

11

Hot, but with some showers. Wind bound. The commander of the *Pio IX* steamer sent to offer to tow us out. The offer was accepted, but no further notice was taken till too late, & then He sent again to say that He had not understood the answer. Humbug!

12

Fine. A little after midday we got over the Bar, not, however, without touching slightly several times. Sea calm, but I was qualmish, for the Vessel rolled from the remains of the swell caused by the Wind of yesterday. We should have got to Trieste in good time, but the Wind lulled when about two leagues off, & we did not get there till the next morning early.

13

Very hot. Went ashore, & passed the morning with Capt. Beddoes, walking about & shopping. His Kindness & Hospitality were beyond bounds, & I had everything aboard that He could give me. Dined at M. Brentano's. In the evening heard the cannon at Venice, 60 miles off! but they could be no where else, & the sound was not to be mistaken. Hotel de France. Bed clean, – all I desire.

Overpowering Scirocco. Trieste quite insupportable. Very stupidly managed to lose from my awkward contrived Pockets a rouleau of 100 Zecs effettivi which I was carrying, with others, to exchange for Paper! a great bore! for now I must take some money. The heat & confusion perfectly bewilder me, after the quiet of Venice.

15

Left at 10 a.m. Very hot, but night chilly. I remembered some of the road; in parts pretty but nothing more, & the green looks cold after Ital^n Brown. Cilli – where the rail road begins – is pretty. Bruck, which had struck me 12 years ago, i.e. – the drive there from Gratz – I did not think much of. The rail road is slow & shaking, & the stoppages, especially near to Vienna, very tedious: so is the passage of the Semmering, where there is a break in the railway. Got to Vienna at 6 a.m. of 17th; very tired & weary & disgusted at travelling without a Servant. To the 'Archduke Charles', clean, but horribly noisy, especially after two years never a night out of Venice. All the accounts from Rome very sad. Ld Ponsonby & my lady in England. The Heat by day insupportable. Took some Seidlitz to cool me. The journey took 44 Hours to accomplish: but the train was a very long & heavy one owing to a quantity of military.

18

I detest Vienna & its climate, & the noise of the carriages drives me wild. The quiet of Venice covers a multitude of sins. Oh! that this madness had never come over the world – especially over Italy – now ruined for my lifetime, & long after. The last *Galignani* which I have seen regularly was of the 19 May.

I must stay here to rest a little till the 20th. How I wish I were in England, & well housed at Coolhurst, with my best & truest friends! I have neither Pleasure nor Interest in travelling any longer. My spirits are not equal to the exertions. Quiet is all I care for. If no war breaks out, I shall return to Venice to my prints & Pictures & Books & reminiscences, probably never to leave it again. Saw Samuel. Good God! It was all of 'Us' & 'We', and a tone much more decided than that of the Ambass^r would have been! How strange a world do we live in!

Went for sights. To the Gallery at the Belvedere. I I think the 'Io' the most beautiful, as well as the most luscious, picture I ever saw. She is lovely, & the expression something overpowering. The Ganymede very pretty, but not to compare. A $\frac{3}{4}$ of a Man in red by Licinio, & a Portrait by Teoscopoli, il Greco, struck me much; a small Giacomo Bassano; a portrait by Titian of a Man with a small figure in his hand, – I suppose an anatomist; two Raffaelles; but everything has been frightfully varnished, absolutely glazed. In the flemish & dutch division the Rubens's are superb; especially a large one, with two side pieces representing, I imagine, some royalties; also two whole lengths in very singular costume: Vandycks very fine: some Teniers, Wynants, Hobbemas, &c, & a very pretty piece by Henri de Cort: two superb Jordaens, and a Hondeschatter. I had no guide book, so cannot remember more. The scent of the Eleagnus Boemica in the gardens here is delicious in the open air. To the Church of les Italiens, where is the mosaic of the Cena of Da Vinci. It is very inferior to those in St. Peter's at Rome, & gives no idea of the beauty of the original.

After dinner drove in the Prater, as far as the Danube, where it bounds the Isle of Lobau. Saw some of the remaining vestiges of the havoc caused by the rebellion here. Alas! how have the peaceable Inhabitants suffered for their supineness!

19

Fine. Paid a visit to Samuel, & saw his *Belle Bohemienne*, who is really very pretty indeed. Then to see the Esterhazy Gallery, some pretty Pictures of the Flemish & Dutch Schools, but too many for pleasure in the whole collection, for you weary with looking thro' much indiff^t for some good. Then to Schönbrunn, the Palms & Ferns very fine. The Orchidacea few & poor, nothing in blossom save a Stanhopea of them. Some fine Achimenes, especially 'picta' red & yellow: a pretty Cufia out of doors. The Palace a handsome building as seen from the Open Loggia above. The young Emperor drove in just as we did. He looked well & cheerful, but passed so quick I could not get a good view of him. They say He is active & has won the hearts of the Soldiers by visiting their barracks &c., & seeing they were well provided for. Then did some shopping; the Glass is very beautiful, & the Carlsbad Porcelain very pretty, quite as much so, or more than ours. After dinner I spoke to Mr. Maginnis who was dining in the same room, in order to explain how I had come to Trieste. Talked to him for some time, & was presented to Mr. Grey. Afterwards drove to see the point by which Windisch Graetz advanced. There are still many vestiges of the destruction committed, especially about the 'Odeon'.

20

As I was to leave in the Evening I did nothing worth recounting. Left by rail for Berlin about 7. The Danube where we crossed it in its width was fine, but the rest of the Journey to Berlin wholly without beauty or interest. The travelling when we got into Prussia was good, the carriages excellent, but the changing from one set to another, & the perpetual stopping very tiresome as you could not sleep tranquilly. It is hard work for one not used to it, & especially without a Servant. However the conductors were civil & obliging, & I managed tolerably. Travelled all the 21st, & got to Berlin between 4 & 5 a.m. of the 22. All the people at the Douanes throughout Austria & Prussia were more civil than any I ever met with, & they did not charge me a penny, or take a fee for not doing so. The 'Hotel Erzherzog Karl' very good in all ways, & very cheap – extraordinarily so. They recommended me to the 'Hotel du Nord' at Berlin, to which I came, & just managed, by waiting for a couple of Hours, to get a good room. Weather so so; chilly & threatening rain. Being weary with two nights travel I did nothing but wander about a little by myself, reserving a *lacquai de place* & carriage for tomorrow. I thought the town dull, though there are many fine buildings, only they are of Plaister not Marble. The present King seems to have aimed at rivalling the ex-King of Bavaria. In the Evening I sent a note to Mr. Howard, & went to the Play House to see Lessing's *Emilia Galotti*; I did not like either the Piece or Emilia's acting; the House, dull, dark & dirty.

Showery. Went to Mr. Howard. I could not retrace
the Boy at Greystoke 25 years ago: but He was
exceedingly kind, & offered & pressed more than I
could accept, namely Introduction to Ld Westmor-
land, &c. By his advice to see Rauch's Studio, and the
monument in progress for the Great Frederic. It is
colossal, and very fine. He has rigidly preserved the
costumes, yet in spite of them & pigtails has succeeded
in conquering the ridiculous. It consists of a colossal
Equestrian figure; on a pedestal, the sides of which
are covered with Bas reliefs of his great Victories. The
colour is that of the Copper Bronze at Munich which
I do not like, tho' probably it shews the figures more
clearly. I went also to the foundery to see the parts
cast. It was to be ready for next year, & to be placed
at the opening of the 'Linden'. Now, God knows
when! There was the model of a table monument
erected at Hanover to the late Queen which pleased
me very much; full of feeling, grace & dignity.

To Statue & Picture Museum. Round the Gallery
which runs round the room where the Statues are,
the King has placed the famous Raffaelle tapestry,
which was bought in London, the English Gov^t being
too stingy to do so. One piece had been destroyed by
the Jew having burnt it for the gold. The Statues
less fine than at Munich. The Picture Gallery rich in
early Italian artists. A Duplicate, slightly varied, of
the 'Io' at Vienna. The Head is lovely, & quite
unlike any other I ever saw by an Italian. I did not
like the whole so well as the Vienna one: there it is
the cloud – here a half distinguished Jove is dimly
visible: a S. del Piombo: a 'Woman in Adultery' by
Pordenone, magnificent. Two Ruysdaels, of a warm

yellow tint very unusual for him, beautiful; a Waterloo, very pretty; a Claude; a S. Rosa; many of the Dutch & Flemish Schools; & a 'Virgin & Child' by Murillo; but the collection is fatiguingly large, & I was not very well: besides, I have lost my notes of what else struck me most. There is a new Museum in progress, a splendid work – how these Germans shame our national Galleries. This new building is destined for the general collection, & is superbly decorated internally, much in the Bavarian taste, & rather too gaudy for mine, but certainly with much effect. There are some remarkably handsome columns of a single block of a black & white marble of Carrara. The model of the great temple of Karnac, I forget in what proportion to the original, but it is very large – is very curious for those who have not been in Egypt. There are other galleries for Egyptian remains painted correctly from the tombs of the Kings, &c. In the gallery of Antiques are some beautiful figures, especially a Bronze statue of Mercury, I think; & there is a superb vase of Agate from the Emperor of Russia: many, many more things which I am too indolent, now, to record, & can scarce remember.

After dinner drove to Charlottenburg; though flat the Gardens are pretty & well laid out & kept, with quantities of flowers. The Chapel, where are the table Monuments of the late King & Queen by Rauch, is the chief thing to see. The monuments are fine, but they still leave you something to wish for. Rauch was a Servant of the Queen Louisa, who observed that whenever she passed thro' the room where he was in waiting, He put away something in a drawer. On examining, she found that they were models, & that he had a great taste for sculpture. He was then turned of 30, but she sent Him to Rome to study, & always patronized Him. He was 14 years at work on the statue of Her which is at Potsdam, & wanted permission to retouch that at Charlottenburg, but the King would not permit it.

Returned & drank tea with the Howards. She is a remarkably elegant & nice person.

Fine. Went to Potsdam by rail, & had for companion Prince Frederick, who talked of different things, & whom I had not a suspicion of. However I said nothing but Loyalty & wishes for the prosperity of Prussia. He is a fine military looking man, quite free from airs, & speaks very tolerable English. At Potsdam saw Garrison Church, where F^k the Great is buried; service was begun & it was full of troops, chiefly Cavalry; fine looking men. Then to the Frieden's Kirche, new & very pretty. Here came the young Prince, son of the Prince Royal of Prussia, a nice looking boy. Then to Charlottenhoff – exceedingly pretty, & the flowers, especially roses, lovely! A copy of the House called the King's at Pompeii restored, in which there is a Vase of Siberian Jasper that is splendid. It is all in very good taste, & perfectly kept. Then to the Neue Palast; a fine building in the french taste. I only walked through it, for I had much more to do, & I am surfeited with Palaces. I only passed through it, therefore, traversing a large circular vaulted Hall, decorated as a Grotto, & handsome.

Then to see poor Queen Louisa's monument. There is a great deal of feeling in the way He has treated it, & the *Sleep* is perfectly expressed: the one at Charlottenburg represents death. But I think that, judging from the cast I prefer that of the Queen of Hanover to either.

Then to Sans Souci, built like St. Cloud on Terraces, & very pretty indeed: all the Terraces were set out with immense orange Trees, & the water works were playing. Here I saw the King, who walked back from Church through the Upper Terrace. He looked dejected: no wonder! Kings have a bad time of it in these days! Then drove to see the Prince of Prussia's Villa at Babertsburg, which is pretty, on the side of a Hill, well cloaked with trees, & looking down on a fine expanse of water. The Architecture is something like that of Rheinstein, castellated. Just by is Glienecke, belonging to P. Charles; much smaller, but very pretty & beautifully kept, as indeed all is. Here are some fine specimens of the *Quercus pyramidalis*, curious but not pretty. All these places a few years back were barren Hills of sand, but now by Irrigation, applied by means of Steam Engines, the sterility of Nature has been conquered.

Then to the Pfanen Insel, where the P. of Prussia took refuge for a fortnight during the tumults at Berlin; for the King would not allow him to act. The House consists of two Round Towers connected together by a gallery, and is of wood. One tower is much out of the perpendicular. Here is a really superb Oriental Hot House, richly ornamented: just what Alessandro Torlonia's should have been. Some fine Palms, & the Gloxinias, blue & white, wonderfully luxuriant. A large garden of Roses, &c., &c. I liked my day much; dined fairly at the Inn, & got back to Berlin, this time having for companion sole (save Raiding) in the Carriage,

Count Brandenburg. He is an unprepossessing Person both in appearance & manner. When I got back I went to the new Opera House to see Schiller's *Jungfrau*. It is not large, but is by far the most beautiful theatre I ever saw, & the Guilding, Painting, &c., most costly & regal.

25

Again to the Picture Gallery, & wandered about without doing much.

26

Do. Saw Mr. Howard again, who sent me to see some modern Pictures at a M. Wagner's. Went to China manufactory. Some pretty specimens. The Copies of ancient Pictures in white porcelain for the Shades of lamps very beautiful, especially Rubens' 'Descent from the Cross'; but there is no travelling with such ware, except in one's own carriage.

27

Went to see the Gallery of M. Wagner, there is the Sacontala, which I remembered at Rome but, except a sketch of a scene in a flat, swampy country, by Lessing, & a Horace Vernet, saw nothing worth mentioning. At night at 10 I started for Cologne. I am well pleased to have seen Berlin, but have no desire to do so again. I am too old for the pleasures & incidents of travel.

When in the Carriage I suddenly agreed with the *lacquai de place*, a former servant of Ld. W. Russell, who had travelled with him & spoke English well, that He should join me at Cologne, & stay with me while I was in England. It will save me the trouble & risk of hunting for one there.

28

Got to Cologne a little before 9 p.m., to the 'Belle Vue' at Deutz. There was nothing on the Journey by Magdeburg, Brunswick, Hanover, &c., save the magnificent Stations of the Railway, which are on the grandest scale. I forgot my geography, &, after leaving Brunswick, went to sleep. Some time after, seeing a town, I asked if it was Hanover; they said, 'No, it was Minden.' We had passed Hanover an hour or two before. I do not suppose the loss was great, but certainly the capital of King Ernest was the only thing I cared about seeing on the road.

At Berlin, 'Hotel du Nord', very fair & people civil; but much inferior in all ways to the 'Archduke Charles' at Vienna. 'Belle Vue' at Deutz dear, dirty, uncivil & detestable.

29

Staid to rest & let my Servant arrive. The Cathedral seems almost at a standstill again for want of funds. The King of Bavaria's windows are beautiful: still the colours are, both in the golden Yellows & Crimsons, inferior to the old. I do not imagine the Undertaking can ever be completed: it is too vast for our times, & revolutions turn the funds to other objects. I went up on the Galleries round the roof outside – a fine view. They seem to finish the new works well & with solidity; but, alas! as they get on since I was there 6 years ago, six centuries will not end it.

A long tiresome day to Ostend, starting about 6½ &
reaching about 9. Went on board & had a rough
Passage of 4 hours & ¼. There was but little pretty on
the journey, except between Liège & some place
with Baths.

July 1

Once more at Dover. I got into the Ship Inn, before
4 a.m. Laid down till the Custom House was opened
& the things passed. There was no difficulty, but the
Commissionaire charged me 10s. 6d. duty for one
quart Bottle of Eau de Cologne, being more than
prime cost!! To London & to Stevens's. Having
cleaned & refreshed, I went across happily to the
Clarendon, & found Lord P[onsonb]ʸ at Home,
about to start for Vienna the next day. What a
pleasure to see Him once more! The greatest I shall
have in England!

2

Lᵈ P. went. I saw the carriage & fourgon packing at
the door. I shall never see Him again, probably! Alas!
For these things is Life prolonged. Weather cold, &
cloudy & uncertain.

3

Same weather. Chaˢ Dickins came to see me.

4

Turned off my Berlin Gent: his accounts not being at
all to my satisfaction. Went to the floriculture show

at the Regent's Park. Some beautiful flowers, especially of the *Aerides*, & some superb Grapes & Strawberries: but there was not the variety of species I had anticipated. Then called on Miss Tilghman.

5

What they call fine in England. My Birthday. Nicely solemnized here in my native land. Called on Gen¹ Hⁿ. Met Lady E. Reynell who was very gracious. Mrs. H. is at Eartham, & it seems very uncertain whether we shall meet. Hired a new Servant for 3 Months at £8 a month, deducting 12s. 6d. a week when we remain a whole week in any private House.

6

Fine.

7

Do. & warm. The Devil is in my ill fortune. The new Valet who came yesterday made his appearance at dressing time this evening dead drunk. So here I am at sea again, & am really almost resolved to do without.

8

Fine. Tried my luck once more. All the sight seeing I have had was the Panorama of Cachemire, and the Mississippi by the American Banvard: neither pleased nor interested me. [*Heavily erased*: 'I sat in the Park; but so shy that I cᵈ make . . . nothing.']

9

Fine. I can't stand the expense, or else one can live well in London, & without going out I have managed not to find time hang heavy. [Last line so much erased that it is quite illegible.]

10

Fine. Came to Coolhurst.

11

Fine.

12

Do.

13

Do.

14

Do. I have in these two days written to Craven & Marino T[orloni][a].

30

The weather has been showery & chilly for the last fortnight. I have done nothing, & am not much amused with the company. But Charles's kindness is above all description. Back to London. Fun & Folly seems the order there for those who have money. [*Erased*: 'Saw J.B. We went up to Albany St.']

32

Same weather, warm but threatening showers, which did not come. To Covent Garden to hear & see *Le Prophète*. It is noisy, but there are some striking pieces, especially the choruses, & Mario's last drinking song. He looked beautiful. If it had not lasted four hours, which is, at least, one too many, I should have liked it all better; but I sat it out, which I have not done for years anywhere, & was rewarded by Mario's last song. [*Heavily erased*: 'I saw J.B. on 3rd & 5th August, & on the 9th & 10th I think but not sure.']

August 4

The weather is grown perfectly wintry & I bilious from taking liberties, I suppose, and forgetting my years. I weighed since I came to England and found myself exactly what I was when I weighed first 40 years ago! and less than I have ever done since, save once. Dined with Mrs. Huskisson.

11

The weather has been sultry, & I stupid & languid. Today dined again (for the last time) with Mrs. H. Miss Tilghman & one of her nieces. Good God! What a 3 hours!!! It was on the 7th that I was ill & had Forbes.

12

[*Erased*: 'J.B. Gravesend.']

13

Water Excursion.

14

Do. and back to Town. [*Inserted later*: '& now on the 6th Septr what regrets & what recollections!!!']

15

[*Erased*: 'Took leave at Kensington. Soon to meet again, I hoped.']

16

To Kinmount. All these days stormy and unsettled weather. The whole road to Carlisle frightful. The train arrived there more than an Hour after its time, so that the Dumfries one was gone, & I had to post at an enormous expense to Kinmount. My journey cost me £8.0.0.

17

Showery & chilly. Lady & Miss Gore came.

18

Do. Do. & I enjoyed a good coal fire in my bed room. Walked to Glen Stuart.

19

Do. Do. To Church at Annan & afterwards walked to Glen Stewart.

20

Cloudy & chilly, but no rain. We went to New Abbey beyond Dumfries & under Criffel: a very pretty ruin.

21

Same weather. The Gores went.

22

Same showery & cold weather.

31

A fine, warm day at last, all the others have been uncertain, if not positively bad. Venice is fallen. Now what shall I do? I burn to stay the winter in England, and, if I can balance my accounts so as to meet the double Housekeeping, I think I must indulge this last fancy, however imprudent such indulgence may be.

September 4

[*So heavily erased as to be quite illegible.*] Yesterday & today fine. Today I left Kinmount, where I found more genuine kindness & affection than I can ever hope to meet with again in any part of the world. God bless my dearest Lady Q[ueensberr]^y. To London, where [*Several pages torn out.*]

December 16

Same; damp, foggy & dirty. Tomorrow I go to Leamington, to my dear Lady Q^y. What thoughts & recollections rise up! On the 16th of August I set out to visit her, leaving my poor Boy strong in Youth & Health, & without a fear but that, 3 weeks past, we should meet again. And now!

I did not leave the House, & the day was weary

enough: – but so they all are now. Would that I had mustered resolution & gone back to Venice as soon as it was over! Would that I had never left it! I feel myself more nervous & more desponding tonight than I have yet done. If I could have the 'Mixture' I think that I could not refrain from trying the 'leap'. My poor boy! Fifteen Weeks back today he was on duty, & taken unwell as tomorrow. Had He then gone into Hospital, instead of drinking to stop it, we might have been now together!

17

Fine. To Leamington. A melancholy journey, for my thoughts turned to the last time I travelled the road, coming from Scotland, in the hopes of many a happy day!

Found Lord & Lady Q. all kindness as ever.

Extract from *The Times* of today:

'In Paris the most fatal month of Cholera was June, when 5,769 perished. In London the most fatal month was September, when 6,644 fell victims.'

18

Wet. Fifteen weeks today since I left Kinmount & since He was taken ill at night; & 18 since we went to Sheerness!! 11 o'clock, P.M. About this hour I was arriving in London, and anticipating our meeting – how joyous it was to be! – tomorrow evening. And I am alive – & He is gone & forgotten save by me – and nothing remains to tell of him save the cold stone which I have had placed by his Grave! How truly I envy him! How gladly would I exchange places with Him! Poor, dear, Boy! My last and best!

Fine. Letters from Canterbury & funny ones. Went to Kenilworth with Lord Q. The ruin much finer than I expected.

20

White frost, sunny but very cold. Called on Mrs. Walker. I was really shocked at the change! & such an account of them all! Drove to Warwick & walked back. The View of the Castle very fine. I left the Interior for some day when alone.

21

Shortest day. Gloomy and dull! Alas for the merry days of Winter which I had dreamed of! My poor fellow! Very cold, with a slight fall of snow. Bowding a very stupid answer.

22

Frost & bitter cold.

23

Do. To Church, such a bad edition of Mawworm I never heard. Alas! I remembered that this day 16 weeks I was at Church likewise with Ld Queensberry, with my last letter to poor Jack in my pocket & thinking of our speedy meeting in joy & in health; & that on the same day He went down in all his beauty, such as I saw Him on the 9th of July, to the Queen's Guard! My own darling boy! Nothing will ever destroy the memory of you! They say that they can find out nothing of his friends or relations. Poor, poor fellow!

24

Cold, wet thaw.

25

Damp, & thaw, but milder. I had reckoned on making a merry Xmas this year! Vain dreams – my joy is gone & I am left to mourn over blighted hopes.

26

Foggy & damp but mild. They took me to Warwick & I walked back, after having seen the Castle, & Mr. Redfearn's curiosity shop. There are a few portraits good in the Castle, but little else to see in the Interior. I forgot some fine *Pietra dura* tables, bought at Venice a few years back. The exterior of the Castle is fine, & the grounds & river must be pretty in fine weather. Very large Cedars. Saw the great Vase too. Mr. Redfearn had some good China, oriental, Sevres, & Dresden & Chelsea, & some agate cups &c: but his things were dear.

27

Dry & Cold. In the evening to Mrs. Walker's. Mrs. Harvey sang & very well. I asked for the drinking song in *Le Prophète*, but she could only hum it over. My thoughts went back to other days when her mother & aunts used to sing; and then the *Beviam* made me feel how much I had lost since the first and only time I ever heard it, on the 31st July. I came home at 11 P.M.

Violent storm this morning early, & the ground covered with snow when I got up. My poor Boy was always longing for the winter & saying how well He should be when the cold came. His bed is cold indeed! The cold overcomes me, & I got up with a presentiment of Ill, & lo! I have broken the crystal of my ring, which fell out. Luckily I found the Hair, which fell likewise. They work so universally ill nowadays, as it seems to me, in England! I would not have lost it for much! My poor, poor boy! I am so weary – so incapable of interesting, or even amusing myself, with anything! If it were not the intense cold I think that I should make an escapade, & try to drown thought & grief in a *vero Baccanale*! There would be found scope enough for even my appetite, I believe.

29

Fine, but very severe frost, which makes me very uncomfortable, & I am, besides, disappointed at having no more letters. My own Boy was so punctual & true & kind! Oh! how I feel his loss more & more daily, & how weary I am of everything! And now, they say so at least, they are coming back to Town –

30

Another Sunday! Cold & no appearance of thaw. I cannot sleep, & can only think of the past, & of how different is the reality of my Xmas & New Year from what I had dreamed of. I am restless & want to be back in London; when there to wish to move again. Would I were at Venice; would, rather, in the grave, where alone I can be at rest. What would have become of me had He lived? I sometimes ask myself this question, & try to draw consolation from considering it – in vain! 17 Weeks today He rode down for the last time in all his Beauty. Oh! what a season this would have been with Him!

31

Cold but with less wind. Drove with L^y Q^y to Guy's Cliff. It must be pretty on a hot day, if ever there is such a thing in these parts. Got two stunners from Canterbury; but, alas! my poor boy! they only serve to make your loss more severe. And now farewell to a year which promised so much, & which has so wounded me. My days of hope, & of pleasure are past, & I look only to closing my days before another 31 December arrives. The recollection of this, & of this visit to England, will embitter every hour to come. My best, & kindest, & truest Jack! May you sleep on in peace for ever! In losing you I lost all that made life valuable, or rather supportable.

1850 Leamington

January 1

Cold, & foggy, & dismal the New Year opens. I pray most earnestly that I may never see the commencement of another. May I soon, very soon, lie in that grave where lie my Joys & Recollections! I am heart sick of everything, & long only for that peace which is nowhere but in the grave. My poor, poor, boy! You should have lived, for you had youth, health & beauty. With you are my recollections of past, my hopes of future, pleasure.

2

Fine morning, but grew raw & inclined for a thaw as we got to London.

3

A nasty thaw, & very disagreeable. A new *desagrément*: my rascally Landlord tells me to quit on the 1st of Feby. I thought I was here till my departure, & had taken the lodging till the 1st April. But it seems there is no written agreement & so a month's notice is valid. Oh Lord! how everything combines to plague me! & how weary & sick I am of all! Would it were finished in any way! I am become too exhausted & too indifferent even to assert my rights, & it is less trouble to change my lodging than to squabble; & so I shall be content with anything.

4

Continued thaw but mild & the air pleasant: the Streets detestably dirty. This thaw, this wet, this dirt, they all make me think of my poor boy. What is he now? Gracious God! Such beauty – & now! The thought makes me shudder! Poor mortality! Why are we here!

5

Fine. I went once more to Brompton & found my poor Jack's grave very neatly kept & not having suffered from the weather. Alas! as I looked at the date of his death, & thought that this very day four months He died! Sleep still, sweet Boy, & may I soon be equally quiet! On this side the grave there is nothing but weariness.

6

A very white frost – very cold & a threatening of snow. I am very low in spirits today; I suppose the effect of the weather, for I have nothing apparently to make me more triste than usual. My annual report of finances is good. Ah! had he lived I might have profited by them! Now I am indifferent, provided I am without debts. Twenty six weeks! (the half year) are complete today, Jack! since I first saw you in Hyde Park! Summer & Winter! the Winter which you so desired – it is here; instead of dust &

Green trees there is the hoar frost & the bare branches! and where are you? I am here still, a solitary wretch – but you have left me for ever! You came as a bright form of gladness, beautiful in youth & strength, & you are now —: while old age & weakness are left to waste away in daily misery! I envy you, Jack, your cold, damp, grave, while I have nothing which you could wish for! Weather or pressentiment or that sorrow which I cannot over-come, I know not which, has made this one of the darkest days that I have felt since the fatal one of his death! If I could have obtained, quietly, the Drug I asked for, in some such day as this has been I should probably have used it: & then – what is the 'then'? Half past ten at night. At last this weary day is finshed, & I go to bed – to sleep? there is the rub. I must try my opiate once more tonight, for I am quite broken down.

7

Fine, but very hard frost. Twenty one weeks today since we made our first – & alas! only – expedition together. Twenty six since we first spoke!

8

Same weather. Eighteen weeks since He wrote his last letter. Six Kalendar months since I first saw him.

9

Foggy & cold & raw. 18 weeks since all was over. Six Kalendar months since we first spoke!!!

> *'Heu mihi! quam sero venio!*
> *Heu! heu! quam tarde festino.'*
> *Med: Sancti Augustini.*

Twenty one weeks since we parted for me to go to Scotland on the next day. How little we either thought that parting would be eternal! Would I had never gone to Scotland. He might have lived had I been here!

10

Snow & hail & rain, the Streets beastly. To crown all in my visit to my *Native* the winter seems to be of the worst description. Oh! my poor Heart! how much has it had, and still has, to endure since I landed on the 1st July!

11

A bitter day; by much the coldest we have had, &, from a partial thaw yesterday & the sudden change to frost, the Parks & much of the Streets are a sheet of Ice. I have chosen a lucky year to winter again in England! Poor Jack! He wished for a cold winter! Would that I had been the one to escape it as He did, & He been left here! I see that Venice is no longer a free port – another difficulty for the things I wished to send out, & a taking away of one of the chief advantages of living there. Would I were prevented the return! Would that I had the courage to prevent it! I know not the use of fire arms: I have not the steadiness for that of the knife or razor, & our purists & philanthropists no longer allow the sale of poison, for the use of which little courage is requisite: *reste* drowning – but there is so much preparation! My poor, poor boy! Your cares are over. May his rest be undisturbed, or if there is that other world, oh! Be all his sins forgiven to Him, & visited on me! All I ask is to leave this weary world!

Another bitter cold day, with snow at times. It is a very severe winter, and, according to me, after a *no* summer; & yet I certainly feel, as yet, the cold much less than at Venice, & have no chilblains. I should have thought that living really alone as I do, & out of spirits as I am, the cold would have been more insupportable; but on the contrary, I can only account for this by the fact that I am become indifferent to everything – for such is the case. I have no pleasure in anything, & my only desire is to close this unprofitable existence, for life it cannot be called, as soon as possible. My poor Boy was the only Interest I had made for myself, & He was taken away! What might have happened had He lived it is now vain to dream of; but He has left nothing behind, & be his loss for good or for evil, I am now all alone in this weary world. For the last ten days, since I came from Leamington, save calling on Mrs. Scott for a quarter of an hour, I have not seen a face I knew, & this in London. On looking back to kill the time this snowy day, I find that, like true human nature, I said but little of those few days since I came to England in which I was really happy. I too confidently hoped that they were only the Introduction to many, many of the same, or even happier; and now that they are gone never to return, I wonder that I should have noticed them so little. What would I now give for one Hour of them back again. There was so much that I had to say, & to ask; so much to be done & arranged! All had been delayed, for an absence of three weeks was as nothing in our calculations.

Same bitter cold. This day, five Kalendar months, we went to Gravesend. Nineteen weeks since He went down to the Horse Guards for the last time! In spite of the cold I could not stay at Home, & I went on the Knightsbridge road to where we parted – for ever. Then to Bⁿ Church yard, & knelt on his frozen grave, & prayed for mercy for him, & that I might soon sleep as He does, & kissed the name on the cold stone which marks the last abode of 'the young, the kind, the beautiful, the brave'.

I have been pondering on which side the advantages were, whether to have relations & friends to whom one was fondly attached, or to be as I am almost alone. If I had the courage to put an end to an existence without charms, I should say that, decidedly, it was better to be alone. Then there would be only the leap to take, and to go unregretting & unregretted. Even as it is with me – i.e. without that courage – I think I have the advantage. If I have nothing to love, I have nothing to consider & am, therefore, freer to act. Would all these thoughts were ended, & that I were in my Grave! Today I am quite beat down, & long to be at rest, for here it is a wearisome daily repetition of sad recollections & nothing to hope for.

The Inscription on poor Jack's tombstone runs thus:

'To the Memory of
John Brand
of the Royal Horse Guards Blues
who died of Cholera
5th Septr 1849,
aged 22.
Implora pace'

14

Cloudy, & the frost one of the most severe known for a long time. It seemed to take fresh force with the new Moon yesterday. Paxton is the name of the man who has got poor Jack's Horse!

15

Same cloudy atmosphere, but the frost increases in Intensity; the cold is almost insupportable; yet I certainly suffer less in Body than I have done at Venice. At any rate here are no Chilblains. My mind, on the other hand, sinks daily under the chilling Influence. Five Kalendar months today since we parted to meet again, as I promised, in 3 weeks! – I never saw him after. Man proposes & God disposes! Who would have imagined such an end! & that his death should be on the very day on which we had fixed our joyful meeting! How well I remember the tone & look with which He used to answer me, when I told him how I loved him, '*I believe you.*'

16

Same intense cold, which seems to be even more severe in the South of France & in Italy.

17

Rather milder & inclined to thaw, I hope. Mr. Milward dined with me. What a fool I was to allow myself to be Trustee to any one, much more to people I cared nothing about. I could not help thinking all the evening what a different guest I had hoped to receive! Alas! Alas!

Cold & damp – neither frost nor thaw, but very disagreeable, and I very much out of sorts. Snow & sleet & rain, so I never moved till dinner at Mrs. Scott's. How these things bore me now! Mary Scott (Dehany) was there.

News from Canterbury. 'The Campbells are coming' but my glorious chief will be wanting! A regular thaw.

Frost set in again, & the Streets sheets of Ice.

Continued frost with such severity that I think nothing can move. There seems a spell against the possibility of doing so!

A partial thaw again. Dined with Mr. Cunningham, & drank too much wine, but it was excellent.

Same weather. Twenty weeks since my poor boy's death!

Same weather. No news of the 'Campbells', who ought to be coming in this thaw. To add to all my

worries the Landlord seems to be a devil, who tor-
ments my unhappy servant in every possible way.
Curse him! For I hate change, & yet it ruins a servant
to have him always tormented below. I am very
bilious, & have walked in the damp these two days
to carry off what, I suppose, are the effects of my
over wining Tuesday, but I am also dumpish &
downish, & more weary of dressing and undressing,
pour tout potage, than I can express.

25

Fine & mild. My damned Landlord has put the
finishing stroke to his Insolence, & so I have had to
take another lodging. I really think that the whole
world is gone mad, & that I am the most unlucky
devil that ever was tormented with Lodgings &
Servants. In the park I had a glimpse of a 'Campbell'
but I was loaded with Oranges & could not stop,
which I afterwards repented of.

26

Showery. What a change! How great is my loss!

27

Fine & clear, with a light frost. To Brompton
Church yard.

28

Cold & rain with sleet. Today the Blues again
mounted Queen's Guard. They went to Canterbury
this day 20 weeks: this day 21 weeks poor Jack came
off guard ill. *Hélas!* Everything makes me more
sensible of his loss. He was something unlike any

other I ever met with. Who was He, or what? They say that no traces can be found of relations, & that it is now supposed that He enlisted under a false name. All this mystery serves to confirm me in the idea I had conceived about him, & which, as I had written him word, I should endeavour to elucidate. He disappeared before an opportunity came. I never saw him again. Perhaps for me it is better thus: – and yet I cannot bear to think so. I should have grown too much attached to him! Poor, poor Boy! He never asked me for a farthing; He was always honourable & good & affectionate.

29

Damp & showery, & I very dismal, for I think constantly of what I have lost. It seems to me that the expression of his eyes when he looked at me sometimes was like that of my poor, poor Beastie, whose large, mild eyes used to watch me with such mute affection! Poor Busy! poor Jack! never shall I find your like! (Either this or the last night I saw Screw first in B^k Bear, without speaking to him.)

30

Cold & raw. My spirits the same; the same regrets; the same longing after the last, long sleep. Would it were come!

31

Same weather, same feelings which gain fresh strength each month, each week, each day. Today I am to go to another lodging; the people here having fairly driven me out of doors. I have nothing to regret in the move, except the trouble, & that is now such a weight upon me that I hardly know how I shall ever muster courage enough for my return to Venice. Would I were there! Would I had never left it! All the sufferings there would have been small in comparison; & *Cholera* might have *killed* me *there*, & not tried me as it has done *here*. Oh! that I had the courage to do the deed! If they would have given me the Acid, I think I could have ended all, but, except drowning, all is uncertain for one so inexpert & unpractised as I. Oh! for a good rapid fever which would do its work quickly & completely! but my health seems to strengthen as my mind & spirits fail. To raise my spirits, it became a thorough wet night. I had to go out for my dinner and to return from it, through the rain, & on coming home found my fire out! My poor, dear Jack, would I were in the Grave with thee! You were the last beam of Sun & Happiness that crossed my path, & with you all is set in darkness & misery! Twenty one weeks today since the Earth received the cold remains of the best & most beautiful Youth I ever knew! How long must I survive to mourn over his memory? How long, O Lord, how long!

February 1

Wet. Dined at the Bedford & to the Lyceum. Booth, I suppose, or Wilford. What a difference from other times. I am grown totally indifferent, & can scarcely feign what I do not feel.

2

My new Lodgings & the Street are dreadfully noisy; and noise is my destruction. How I long to be back at Venice, now that I have nothing to do here. Weather showery, but mild. They say the winter has been dreadful at Venice, as well as all over the continent.

3

Fine, & saw the sun again at last. A fortnight now, & no answer from Gratwicke; So – so – there is an end of that! Went to the Church yard at Brompton; would I were lying there with poor Jack. I am well nigh worn out with all these blows; though, after all, I care little for them. My heart is dead, and I feel nothing now, but the increasing weariness of life & all belonging to it.

4

Fine, but I feel that something is coming, & I repent me that I have not coined an Illness, & sent my excuses to Slindon; for I have a vague sort of belief that it would be better not to go there.

5

Fine. My weariness grows more oppressive, & I long for that repose, which yet I have not the courage to seek by my own hands. How gladly would I know that tomorrow should be the 'be all & end all' of my existence! My sole wish now, if I must live on, is to find myself again in my own apartm^t at Venice. Twenty five weeks since we went to Sheerness; 22 since he wrote me his last lines! Wet night, & storm of wind. Oh! how unlike everything is to him! How every fresh trial proves to me more & more that He was a thing apart. Alas! alas!

Tonight I went to see an old chum of his, Paxton. He seemed really to have loved my boy, and to regret him, and knew more of him: but He was so drunk, & unwell from an attack of English Cholera, that I could make out but little. Yet I felt a kindness towards him, for his manner of speaking of my poor Boy.

6

Stormy & threatening. Heard from Lady Newburgh, Lady Q., Mrs. H^n & from Gratwicke. It seems I had omitted to put my address on my letter, & he never thought of asking at Stevens's. So one thorn is removed for the present: but then I have another *desagrément* sprung up in King. Had a pleasant half hour after parade & made some new, rollicking acquaintance.

7

Uncertain & cold like March. Rather a pleasant evening with my yesterday lads – or rather with two of them – rare boys, by God! & no mistake; but for gentleness & *simpatia* nothing like my own poor boy, who has no equal left.

8

Cold & cloudy. Repetition of evening party: two prime swells in their way; but the fun is expensive, & yet there is no grudging the blunt to such roaring boys.

9

Wet & windy. To Slindon. Mrs. Ravenhill & dau^r & Sir G. Walker staying there. The Haslers & Mr.

Tierney & Mr. Caruthers dined. Pleasant, & My Lady all kindness & so wonderful!

10

Fine. Walked to Eartham with Sir G. Walker. Mrs. H. at church. De la Feld came.

11

Wet & stormy. Mrs. H. &c., dined.

12

Same weather. Lady N.'s birthday. The last on which I shall ever see my kind Hostess, most probably. 26 weeks since Sheerness; 23 since his last note! *Eheu! eheu!*

Visits for the Birthday: among others, C.C. If I could now feel anything I should have felt his conduct. But now all is over for me, & I am alike insensible to pleasure or pain, Kindness or Slight: all I long & pray for unceasingly is the peace of the grave: and that, alas! comes not. I wish I dared seek it! Would not drowning do? Such is the question I now often ask myself.

After dinner, or rather at 9 o'clock, we had some singing in the Hall, & a bowl of Punch. Drury sang, 'Begone, dull care' & all joined in Chorus, the all being Lady Hunter, Mrs. Ravenhill & daughter, Sir G. Walker, De la Feld, the Priest & self. It was a strange & melancholy scene, for I shall never join it again, even if the good Hostess's life be prolonged to another anniversary. Strange & melancholy – past, present & future!

13

I could not sleep a wink all night. A fine day & we separated never to meet again! The kind Countess quite a wonder. God bless Her! I think Sir G. Walker the nicest & most *simpatico* young man I ever met with. Walked to Eartham & was well received; but I am quite knocked down, & can with difficulty keep up spirits enough to make a decent appearance. Would to God I were in the Grave! Next to that wish is the one to be at Venice in my own domicile: but if death would come & save me the weary exertion of getting there – Oh! how joyfully would I hail him, my deliverer! I cannot express the loathing which I have of Existence. Six months today (Kalendar ones) since on the 13th of August we went to Gravesend! And I am here, never to know joy again, till the last Hour is come!

14

Wet all day. The melancholy and desolation of this House & all belonging to it are sufficient to depress any spirits: &, besides, I am unwell, more so than for a long time. Mrs. H. talks incessantly, but does nothing else.

15

Wet & foggy. 6 Kalendar months today since I took leave of my poor Jack, in hopes destined to be frustrated. Alas for me, not for him! This way of life wearies me past bearing, & I long to be back in London, with some excitement. Dined alone at the Haslers; a Party of 19, & pleasant. I had never been there since the days of poor Lady H.H. It was all so different.

16

Fine. Lady Newburgh called.

17

Cloudy & cold. Strange 1st Lesson at Church.

18

Fine. To Ham. Yesterday it was 32 weeks since I first saw Jack: today 32 since I first spoke to him: 29 since we first met together of an evening: 27 since we went to Gravesend: 24 since He was taken ill with Cholera!

19

Cloudy. As I buttoned on my boots this morning I remembered that this day 27 weeks I helped him to button his!

20

Wet. Walked to Arundel. 24 weeks since he died. Saw the Corneys. Sent letter to Craven & to Tom.

21

Fine. Walked to Lady Hunter's.

22

Do. & hot. Walked to Lady Pechell's.

23

Fine.

24

Do. but cold.

25

Cloudy. To London. As I reached the London Bridge Station, it was just 28 weeks since we had arrived there to go to Gravesend. Oh! my poor Boy. There is none like you: every trial I make proves more & more that nothing can replace or equal you! Poor, poor Jack!*

26

Fine. Twenty five weeks He wrote his last letter! twenty eight & we were at Sheerness! Oh memory! Dined with Mrs. H^n to meet the Wilds. Mrs. H. well & in spirits.

27

Fine. Went to see the 'Nile'. Exhibitions bore me now. My poor boy! I have thought all day of you.

28

A heavy fog, so that I can scarce see to read at midday.

March 1

Very fine. I went to see Messrs. McCracken, as a first step towards my last journey. Would it were all over, or that it might end here! At night I saw my poor Jack's two chums. Poor, dear fellow!

* I dined in the Haymarket on this day.

2

Cold March day.

3

Do. Very cold.

4

Do. Do. Some sport all these days, & one may have plenty of fun.

5

Same cold March weather.

6

Fine but same. Six & twenty weeks today, six Kalendar months yesterday, since my best boy died. Peace be with him; his memory will last as long as I live! It grew quite warm after midday.

7

Very mild. Went to Brompton Ch: Yard!!! Reading *Le Vicomte de Bragelonne* a novel by Dumas today I fell on the following passage – a curious coincidence!

    '*Le 5 Septembre! dit elle; oui, ma douleur a paru le 5 Septembre. Grande joie un jour, grande douleur un autre jour. Grande douleur, ajouta-t-elle tout bas, expiation d'une trop grande joie.*'

8

Fine but foggy.

9

Do. David Young!

10

Do. Real March weather.

11

Do. D. Y. no good.

12

Do.

13

Do. Oh! my poor Boy! Every day makes your loss more bitter.

14

Foggy, & I with a bad cold.

15

Do. I have been quite quiet these two days, without going out, in doubting expectation.

16

Do. bitterly cold. Went (I little thought I should ever have the courage to do so) again to Gravesend with D. Paxton (poor Jack's chum & whom he christened Screw). He is a nephew of Paxton at Chatsworth; a very good fellow, & much attached to the memory of my poor Boy. The day was in March much the same as its predecessor in August, cold with rain, &c.

17

Bitter cold. We had the same Rooms & Champagne & —; but my poor Boy! there is nothing that I can ever love as I did you. We dined & back to Town by the last train, which did not leave till past 8. I hope He was in time at Home!

18

Same piercing weather.

19

Showery.

20

Cold. I am returning to a weariness & depression which I try in vain to struggle against. Oh! how I long to be at rest! How I envy my poor Boy his grave.

21

A cold, thick fog. A melancholy day to me! Called on Mrs. H. & took a last leave, probably. I was cold – she, on the contrary, seemed rather softened. That Episode of my life is over! Then to poor Jack's Grave, & my tears fell for Him, as I envied his quiet repose, far away from the griefs & disappointments of this weary life. At night I was fairly beat out of patience. Drunken brutes! How was it that poor Jack was so different from all others.

22

Showery & uncertain. I breathe, but can scarcely say that I exist. I know not when I have suffered so much

depression as today. I want to be back at Venice, &
yet I feel as if the effort to start will be impossible. I
leave here such recollections!

23

Snow in the morning. Mr. Paxton called in the
Evening!

24

Bitter cold with Snow. Sunday. I tried to see & hear
the Band, but it did not come down to Chapel. The
last time I heard it was in 1843, the morning I embarked: then I saw G. Wilcocks who now lies in the
same grave with my poor boy – upon his coffin! – I
must go, for I am dying here by inches & can bear it
no longer. I must make the leap & go, either back to
Venice or to the bottom of the Thames. Would I
were in Brompton Church yard! I can bear this life
no longer. The day I return from Coolhurst I will
begin my preparations, & get away as soon as possible. Till I am across the water I shall not breathe
freely: shall I then? there's the question. Yet here I
cannot stay: – such a day as this – such days as the last
week has brought – I cannot bear – & yet nothing
has occurred out of the usual routine: but I am so
weary of everything – so utterly indifferent to all, that
I must get back to my own den at Venice, where, at
least, every day will not bring back such overwhelm-
ing recollections! My poor, poor Boy!

25

Fine but very cold & with snowstorms. To Coolhurst. It was a pleasure to walk again in the free air;

& to see friendly faces; but the thought rose that 32 weeks ago today *we* went to Gravesend: & my heart sunk; and then the talk of my dearest L^y Q. & the same fears & same dread for what may be her future fate! Would I were removed from this weary world. I went & prayed in the Church Porch for the dead & the living! Would I were quiet in that Church yard: but I have yet, I fear, long years of suffering in store.

26

Very severe frost in the night. Day fair till evening, then sleet & threatening change. Walked with Charles. 37 weeks today came here, after having made acquaintance with Him the day before. 32, at Sheerness together. 29, His last letter written that 'He was all right again!'

27

Very cold & gloomy, like December. 32 weeks are passed since I took leave to meet again in joy in three short ones. Twenty nine are gone since, instead of that meeting, He breathed his last! Would to God I could do so, for neither Joy or Hope remains for me. Now I only long for death, or to be quiet once more at Venice, to weep in silence over the memory of poor Jack!

They say that a nice House in Horsham was sold the other day for £400, & was immediately let for 3 years certain for £40 a year; also one at Lewes, with Garden, sold at same price. Would I not do well to make such a purchase & settle here in England? If my poor boy had lived, then – & what then! I now, at least, have no courage to take any such decided step. We walked to Den Park.

28

Very fine, but 10 degrees of frost in the night. 29 weeks since He was laid in the cold ground, unmourned, unknown & forgotten! At least one friendly heart has placed there a memorial of Him, & marked the spot where lies all that is left of Youth, Strength & Beauty. Took a long walk with the Dickins's.

29

Still very cold. Good friday. To Church. Wind veered South, but same frost, & cold.

30

High wind. I walked to Horsham. Screw. At night a little rain.

31

Wet. 30 weeks today since He went down to his last Guard! In 3 I shall be gone for ever from all that was of him, save his Memory!

April 1

Showery but quite mild with a Southerly Wind.

2

Very fine. A warm spring day, such as ought to make glad those whose hearts are not cold and dead. Thirty weeks today He wrote me his last, while I was coming up from Scotland, impatient for tomorrow evening! Such are our hopes & plans here! I think I shall linger on till Tuesday the 30th – and then farewell, most likely for ever.

3

Showery. Thirty weeks since He closed his eyes for ever & my Heart ceased to know joy.

4

Showery. To London. Shall I ever see Coolhurst or its kind Inhabitants again!

5

Fine. Began to think of preparations & sent letter to Antonio at Venice.

6

Showery. I went again to the Church Yard where the poor boy sleeps. Alas for me! At night Screw did not come as He had promised. I cannot guess why –

7

Very fine. No tidings of Screw. I am much puzzled at his not keeping his word last night, or not coming to-night. Alas! for my own Jack! who never broke his word. It is singular that for the first time (with the exception of Mr. Leeves the clergyman at Athens) I saw my name spelt as we do, on a tomb stone in Brompton Church yard yesterday: – it was 'George Charles Leeves Jackson.' I would be well content if 'Edward Leeves' were on a stone there next week!

8

Gloomy & showery. I am very uneasy, for I can hear, or see, nothing of Screw, &, besides that He is a bold, audacious blackguard, such as I like, He is a kind of recollection of my poor boy. I puzzle myself till I grow nervous, to imagine what has happened. Saw McCracken and made sundry preparations for going. And now would I were gone. Poor Screw is ill and going into Hospital. He says Haemorrhoids – who knows: but, like poor Jack, He never asks for anything. Shall I see him again? Poor Jack! Poor me, rather. If I begin to be fond of any one, something is sure to befall him. I had anticipated some fun & pleasure this week & next, & now all hopes are again blighted!

'To lose a friend, & feel that there can be no return, not even for one short hour, through all the coming months, & seasons, & years, of life, no word, no glance, no token of forgiven wrong, of continued love, of hoped reunion; to know this dreadful truth, to feel it pressing heavily upon a heart yet unused to its vacancy, this is misery indeed.' *The King of the Hurons*, an American novel by Putnam.

9

Weather uncertain. I did nothing but make some preparatory purchases. Mrs. Sabine came to see me.

10

Very fine. Had good tidings of the sick & hope to see him tomorrow. Went to British Museum. The Nineveh antiquities very curious: they are in low relief, & something between Indian and Egyptian I suppose.

11

Showery. Preparatory purchases. In the evening Screw came to see me.

12

Stormy, thunder & lightning. Poor Jack's first Reg^t was the 72 Highlanders. Poor Boy! I trust that He sleeps well! At night T. Roberts.

13

Showery. To Gravesend with Screw.

14

Doubtful morning, but it was pleasant after 1 o'clock, & we strolled about. Something disturbed my inside, & I but just got into my Home at 10¼ P.M. in time. I was worried all night with a sharp attack of Cholerine, I suppose. It was provoking to attack me so, for we lost an hour & a half of good company.

15

Wet. Two weeks more & I quit this Place & these scenes. And now, my poor Jack, I shall never again visit Gravesend, which is endeared to me by the Memory of you. There is nothing left like you, Jack, for beauty or for gentleness. Would I were with you now in the grave. Screw is a good fellow & has behaved perfectly towards me, but I cannot feel towards him as I did towards my poor Boy. I am suffering today, & my spirits feel the effect of Illness; but still more they are depressed by the feeling that all now will soon be finished for ever: – all except existence – and how long is that to endure!

My last visit to Gravesend has been precisely for the corresponding days – 13 & 14 – of the month – which I passed in my first visit there with my best Jack eight Kalendar months ago – August & April!

Wet. I feel very poorly & sad both in mind & body. Went to the mediaeval exhibition in the Adelphi, which has been over puffed, I think. After having seen the collections abroad this was poor in comparison. Screw gives no sign. How different poor Jack would have been!

17

Uncertain. It struck me this morning that it was on the eighth July I first saw Him: & on the eighth of September I first saw His Grave, where He had then been placed three days, or rather it was the third, for He was carried there on the sixth.

Called on Mrs. Smith, & made some preparatory purchases. In the evening Screw came to see me. Strange! He tells me that his father has sent to say He will buy his discharge, & that in three weeks he will, probably, no longer be a 'Blue'. Thus then within the year – within the period which I have passed in England, of the only two I have cared about one is dead, the other has quitted!!! and I go to die, soon I hope, in a far distant land!

18

Same weather. More preparations – more melancholy letters – and my spirits sinking, sinking. Yet why should I wish to stay here? Oh! that I were at my home in Venice, or in that last Home for which I long so truly! How weary, oh! how weary is this existence! To Brompton Church Y^d once more. Poor Boy! his Grave looked decently kept, but there is none to mourn for Him but myself – 'By all forgotten.'

19

Wet all day – which is inconvenient now that I am really finished up. Heigh Ho! poor Jack.

20

Same weather. I feel more weary & more incapable of exertion every day, & I shall not be better till once more established in my solitary home at Venice: then forgotten, but not forgetting, I must wait longingly for the hour that will lay me in the grave. It is but uncomfortable lying at SS. M. & C. – but what signifies. Still I would rather be in Brompton Ch: Y^d by the poor boy.

Today I went to see the House of Lords. It is fine, but I did not much like the Kings & Queens; the painted Glass was so same & monotonous. As to the frescoes I could hardly see them & they did not strike me as very remarkable; but I was too far off to judge them fairly. Saw Screw tonight & Tom R. last do.

21

Same unsettled April weather. Saw Screw for an hour.

22

Fine but chilly. Did Arctic Region Panorama & Garden at Regent's Park, & got Passport. How weary I am of all & everything. I almost wish all my things at Venice had been destroyed & then I should not have had the trouble of going back – But then! – Better, perhaps, as it is: but better, far better that I were dead. Yet I have not the courage or energy to take the leap. If I had the Prussic Acid I think that at some moment I should swallow it. Whilst in the Hort[l] Garden at Regent's Park today I remembered that the last time I was there was at an Exhibition on the 4th July. The bands of the Household troops were there. Then I had never seen my poor Jack! Would I had never done so! How much sorrow I should have been spared!

23

Gloomy & chilly like Nov[r]. I want to be gone; for every day I imagine some fresh difficulty, & my courage sinks. In leaving England before, it has always been in comfort, with a Carriage and an experienced Servant, & though, perhaps, the last time I did not acknowledge it, always with the thought of returning. Now I have nothing left here that can wish to see me again & little which I would care to see, & I go without Hope or Interest for the future. Had Jack lived I should, very possibly, have done something foolish with regard to Him. Now I care for nothing in that sense. I try to think that his death has removed a great danger, & that I ought to reconcile myself in that thought; but it is of no use, for I loved the Boy – What He might have proved on longer acquaintance matters not now. I found him without fault, & I love to imagine that He would have continued the same throughout.

Paid a farewell visit to Miss Tilghman; in going there met Mary Scott & Eliza Dehany. At night Screw sent an excuse, so that I lost an evening, & I go on the 30th for I am so wretched here, that anything is preferable.

24

Chilly but fine. Met Charles Dickins & the boys. They tomorrow to Antwerp – He to the funeral of the D^{ss} of Marlbro°'. I went once again to see my poor Jack's grave. It is decently kept. They say no further interments will take place if the new Bill passes, but that nothing will be moved or displaced now existing, especially where the ground has been paid for. So I trust my poor boy's remains will be undisturbed. Yet, except to myself & my feelings, what would it signify? He is insensible to such things, & there seems no one but myself to remember that *He* ever lived! Screw came in the evening, but the contrast is too great between Jack & any other. I am low, but am now eager to be gone, & altogether something more reconciled.

25

Cold & gloomy as if November were come again. I think that I have now completed my purchases & done all I have thought of doing latterly since my courage failed me to make excursions for sightseeing – Chatsworth – Kew, &c. Had he lived I doubt whether I should have mustered courage to go, or I should have bought his discharge, or committed some folly; that is, had our Intimacy endured, & I will not believe, or even imagine, that I should not have loved him more the more I knew him. He has left the Impression, at least with me, that He was one of those rare & bright spirits which we so seldom meet with. To me He was the most *simpatico* person I have known. Strange that no Letters, no Inquiries, have been made or received, & that no clue exists of who his friends are!

Went to the Zoological G^{ns} in the Regent's Park. The day was not favourable, for it was foggy & cold, but, altogether, I think it is the thing best worth seeing here. The Giraffes were superb – 6 of them – & in high Health. A Toucan – and the reptiles very fine. At night to hear *La Donna del Lago*. I had not seen it since the days of Sontag & Curioni, when Mrs. H. had a box, & it was a standing dish of the season. Grisi looked too full & matronly for Ellen, & was ill dressed: Mario was a grand FitzJames, & Tamberbici an excellent Roderic. But the performance went off rather coldly, & the music is feeble. Instead of repeating the '*Aurora al' songerai*' behind the scenes as Curioni used to do in the last Act, Mario sang a beautiful air & was encored, '*Io ti viddi*'. After it they gave two acts of Massaniello. The quick movement in the overture recalled to me that the last time I heard it with a band was in August 1843, on the Sunday morning before I embarked for Antwerp. I went to Hyde Park corner to see the Blues march by to Church, & their Band played this. There & then I saw for the last time George Wilcox, who died on the same day, & now lies in the same Grave, with my poor Boy. Jack is undermost, & on his Coffin that of Wilcox! Would mine were the third! My Heart is heavy, & will never know any other feeling now than one of weary melancholy. Yet I must live on, from the pure cowardice of not knowing how to finish an existence which daily becomes more irksome. My only Hope now is that, arrived at Venice, I may sink into a state of apathetic Indifference, and become capable of tolerating quietly the monotony of my days. No sun can cheer them, but may those that remain – oh! may they be few! – pass undisturbed by further cares.

26

Fine, but chilly. Now having finished all, I am impatient to be gone, though it is going, probably, for ever. Would that the 'Be all & end all' had closed here, & that I had laid my Bones where those of poor Jack moulder! But no – nothing seems to take effect upon my Body. I have exposed myself to all chances, & my life seems a charmed one!

27

Fine but very cold, with a strong easterly wind & clouds of dust. I have put off my departure for a few days, & dine with Mrs. Smith on Tuesday. By this delay I shall see either Sontag & *La Sonnambula*, or Mario & Grisi in *Les Huguenots* on Thursday. I think I shall go on Sunday, but must wait till Tuesday to see the Time tables for May before I can decide. Chas Dickins called this evening, but I was out. Strange that I hear nothing from Screw, since Wednesday, when he went away suddenly saying He was unwell. I have made several new Acquaintances, so that a few days delay may be amusing. Later received a nice letter from Screw with a button, all right. He & Tom do look stunning in their White Leathers!

28

Same cold March like weather. Today saw Screw on his last Guard! In the evening with T.R. to Paddington!!!

29

Same bitter weather. Screw (the last time I ever saw him) came in the Evening. What a set of fellows these Blues are!

Same weather. Called on Mrs. H., who was very low. Afterwards Bill Thompson – a rollicking Yorkshireman of prodigious gifts. Then dined with Mrs. Smith, which I found vastly dull.

May 1

Inclined to be showery, but still a bitter N. Easter, & I not at all in good order. At $8\frac{1}{2}$ a.m. the Queen produced another prince, & is doing well. The cold has completely knocked me up, & I hardly remember feeling anything so intense. Consequently I really could not keep my tryst tonight, for I am unwell besides the cold, & could neither drink, smoke or make merry. Yet I am sorry to lose an Evening now that the last is so near. Poor Jack! I doubt whether I should ever have had the resolution to go, had He been living. Poor, Poor boy!

2

Finer but very cold. Wrote to Craven. Went for the last time to Brompton, 34 weeks since He was laid there! How as I looked on the grave I wished to be there too! 4 P.M. One of them (it was Thompson told me) has just told me that Screw had bought his discharge and left on *Tuesday*. He was here on *Monday* evening, & agreed, if he could get leave, to go to Hampton Court as tomorrow. I have not seen, or heard from Him since: so that it may be true, for he ment^d having had the money for his discharge, but that He had sent it back. This seemed strange; but, if He is gone without seeing me, it is only another proof that with poor Jack I lost all that was good &

true. However this report (probably a true one) has made me sad, & still more weary of everything. I saw him in full dress on Sunday last, & when He came off guard on Monday morning. There is no *truth* left in the world, & people lie without reason or advantage. Folly & danger of procrastination. Had I gone on Tuesday, as was settled, I should not have had this mortification, for such it is, for the moment, though it will be salutary in its effects, perhaps, in various ways! Only would I were dead; whatever may be beyond the grave, I shall never be fitter for my judgment than I am now, and I am so weary.

At night I went to hear *Les Huguenots*, but was rather disappointed: there was nothing equal to the drinking song in *Le Prophète*, & it is too long. I thought, though I hardly expected it, that I might find a letter from Screw at my return; but there was none. So it is true what I heard in the morning, & He is gone without a word! *Pace per me! oh! Signor!*

3

Fine & Sunny, but still the air very cold. I could not sleep & got up low & dejected. Yet it is, I believe, best as it is. I might have committed some imprudence about writing, & that might have produced difficulties. Besides, though He deceived me, He came to see me the last night that He was 'a Blue', and He may have good reasons, as He thinks, for breaking off any further Intercourse. He might fear my Indiscretion. And now all is over. He was the last living recollection of poor Jack - the only one of his comrades who seemed to remember Him! Poor Jack! his cares are over! poor Screw! his probably to commence! May He be lucky & prosperous, whatever

He may have become! He always behaved well &
honorably to me, except not telling me the truth on
the evening of Monday the 29th April, when he came
to me for the last time, & Got his discharge the next
day. He should have written a line; for the plan to go
to Hampton Court as today was his own proposition.
And now farewell to the Blues! Jack is dead! Paxton
gone! My last present to each was a knife - one of ill
omen, & so it has proved: the last of each to me a
Button! Strange recollections these! Where is He
gone? Home to Wimbledon? or to be married at
Canterbury? or to some situation? This is what I shall
never know.

When I came in at night I found a short letter from
Screw come by the last delivery. It was not written
in good spirits, I think, but it is true that he is going
to be married! He says no more but that & that He
had left the Reg^t but begs me to write, which I did
& posted it before I went to bed. He is an honest
fellow, but never was what poor Jack was in my
eyes. He will, I doubt not, make an honorable man
in whatever line he takes up; but the gayest &
merriest days of his life are, I fear, gone, passed among
the Blues. I should like to have seen him once more;
but it is a very great satisfaction to have heard. I was
quite vexed at the idea that He had forgotten me
quite & so soon. Now I long more than ever to be
off, & to be at *Venice* – for I cannot say *Home*; I have
none, never shall have save the *Grave*: would I were
there!

4

Milder but cloudy, as if the rain were coming. In the
morning wrote again to Screw. I am very nervous,

&, as ill luck, or rather bad arrangement, will have it, shall reach Paris, I believe, the very day of the celebration of the republic!

'*Qu'auriez-vous fait de plus pour un ancien ami? J'aurais probablement fait moins, me répondit-il. Les anciens amis, on les connaît trop bien, et alors on les laisse se tirer d'affaire aux-mêmes.*'
Un Capitaine de Beauvoisis, par le Marquis de Foudras.

Wet so that I was driven in this morning. Called on Mrs. Hⁿ. She was more kind in her manner than usual now, & made me promise to write when safe arrived at Venice; talked, too, of my coming to live in England! Why should I? for what pleasure? Shall I reach my journey's end? If I believed in presentiments I should say, 'No.' If death would come, welcome, thrice welcome. I feel that, at any rate, I can regain no quiet or tranquillity till I am at Paris. There, perhaps, the novelty & change of scene may distract me, & act favorably on my nerves. At present I am ashamed of myself, yet cannot wrestle against the melancholy that overwhelms me. Two days more & I am set rolling, & then I would hope to rally a little. At night another letter from Screw, & a very kind one.

5

Milder, but looking unsettled. Went before Breakfast to see the Blues mount guard; my last view of them! Last Sunday I saw Screw among them; the last guard He mounted. Afterwards a farewell, most likely an eternal one, to poor Jack's grave. He died exactly 8 Kalendar months ago today! I went into the Church, where there was service, & tried to pray for him.

Poor boy! cut off in the very flower of youth & beauty, & I old & worthless & miserable left here to drag on a weary existence! In the afternoon went down & took leave of Tom Roberts. Poor fellow! my going will be a loss to him too! He looked so clean, & so smart! It is the finest reg^t certainly in the world.

Yesterday I saw the Swallows for the first time this year. A wet evening & I had no spirits to go out; besides Screw had talked of calling, but he did not. It is better so, yet I had a weakness to have seen him once again. Now then all is finished! Well – let it be so! Let me say with the Italians – *Pazienza!* All I pray for is that the curtain may soon drop! Tomorrow, & I leave London, probably never to see it again! The next day, & I quit England probably for ever! Would that I had laid my bones there! My last week has been a sad one! and yet I ought not to blame Screw, &, at least, I have written to him in kindness.

6

Very wet. Wrote last night, & again this morning, to Screw. He neither came nor wrote. Gratitude! or perhaps He is closely watched & engaged. But I am such a fool that I feel hurt, for I had thought better of him. *Pazienza!* Man is man! Started from terminus at $1\frac{1}{2}$ & got to Folkestone before 6. A Hurricane all night, cold & wet, so that I was glad to have decided on staying there. A melancholy day, for I thought of last Monday, & of Screw's last visit, & our last sherry. Screw in a certain way seemed to recall Jack, & I was growing very fond of him. Would I were dead! would I had never returned to England, or had laid my bones there. To bed at 9, sick & sad & weary.

7

Tuesday. Wet & stormy till after midday, so I waited.
At that hour it gleamed warm & I went to ramble on
the cliffs & to think of Jack & Screw & the gay
Blues. All gone now! As it seemed very doubtful
whether by crossing tonight I should be in time for
the late train I determined to wait till tomorrow
morning.

8

Wet morning, but we got over pretty well, in rather
less than 3 Hours. I was not sick but suffered from my
usual malaise. Adieu England & my bold Blues! Is it
for ever? As far as larking with them – Yes. Poor
Jack! your troubles are over! Screw, yours probably
to begin, for this will never turn out well, I fear – &
I only look to the Grave for rest! All pleasure lies
buried with my dear Jack. Had he lived, what folly
should I have committed! I regret not having seen
Screw once more – yet now it would have been all
the same. No trouble with the Custom House. A
nasty cold showery day, & I wretched. Dined at
'Hotel des Bains', & got off a little after 9 P.M. and
was through the Douane at Paris a little after 5 a.m.
I never saw greater civility from all. I had a carriage
entirely to myself, & thought of poor Jack & Screw!

9

Cold & showery. Could get no rooms at Meurice's,
nor at Hotel Bristol, nor at Mirabeau, so came to the
Wagram. I hate Paris, and am already tired of it.
Wrote to Screw, & insisted upon hearing. Dined at
Very's. Inclosed a half £5 to Screw; perhaps this
may provoke an answer!

10

Same uncertain weather. Wrote to Teresa. Ten months ago yesterday I went to the Horse Guards & saw poor Jack go down in full dress, & afterwards spoke to him for the first time. I never saw him in his full dress after. The 8th (the day I left England) was exactly eight months after I first visited his grave & saw where all his youth, beauty & worth lay! Would I were there with you, my best & dearest Boy! After you, Jack, life has no more joys for me! Screw, too, is married & has cut his old friend – may He never feel the want of him! Yet I fear for his prosperity, & that his marriage (if he is married) will be his ruin. He will run away some day to America, I apprehend. What strange coincidences! On the 8th July I first saw Jack; on the 8th Septr I first visited his grave; on the 8th May I left England, probably never to see it again. Yet I did well, for when Screw was married all my ties were broken. It is strange, here is another day without a letter from him. Shabby fellow! And Chas Dickins is silent too. I would give anything for a letter from Screw, & feel that till I get one I shall be restless & fidgetty. I think, if he gets that which I sent yesterday, he will surely write.

M. de Kermainguy came to see, but He is going into Belgium tomorrow. I do not quite know whether I am glad or sorry. I have no longer any spirits for gaiety. Dined again at Very's. Eating & drinking is all that I can find to do at Paris. They threaten fresh disorders from day to day. I will be off the end of next week.

11

Same uncertain weather, but rather more springlike

feeling, & the people begin to shew in the Gardens. Went to the Louvre, but the Gallery was all in confusion, & I not in a humour for admiring anything. Again a day & no letter from any one! Dined at Defour's, which I did not find so good as Very's.

12

Cloudy & uncertain. This day week I saw the glorious Blues go down to the Queen's Guard for the last time, & saw Tom Roberts in the same box where I first spoke to my ever dear Jack! Poor Tom! I sent him a little canary from Folkestone. The blackguards will miss me sometimes. Oh! that blasted Screw! If I could have a letter from him, I should feel comforted. This day week, too, was my last visit to my poor Boy's grave: & tomorrow nine months since we went down together to Gravesend, in the full & confident hope that it was only the first of many, many other like frolics! Today I got a letter from Screw, a very nice one. Poor fellow! I hope he will do well! As far as I can make out he had not got my letter of the 9th when he wrote: so I hope to hear again on Tuesday. He is a true & good fellow. Dined again at Very's. Anything so triste as Paris I never saw! What a change! In the evening I walked in the Champs Elisées, but all was dull. The obelisk is fine, but the accessories detestable. The fountains fine as compared to ours in London, but sadly inferior to those of St. Peter's; the lower jets are good, but the upper one merely bubbles out, instead of rushing up into the air. I cannot admire *l'arc de triomphe*, & as for the sculpture it is worse than French even usually is. The obelisk spoils the view of the *Arc*, by cutting it, but the *coup d'oeil* is fine. The Madeleine detestable.

13

A wet day. We have not had a fine one yet in this month. I was in hopes, rather, to have heard today that my half-note, sent on the 9th, had been received. Sent off the rem^r today and a cheque for £10 for a watch as a wedding present. May He be happy & steady: though I doubt: he is too wild & daring for common life. No letter from Charles Dickins. Is he ill, or has he, too, got some crotchet? A thorough wet day, & I thought all the while of nine months ago! Dined at *Les 3 frères*, which is the best. I meant to have gone to hear *Le Prophète* for the sake of 'the Brindisi', but it was so wet I could not, & perhaps it is better to rest with the recollection of Mario. When I heard him, I was to see my best & dearest Jack the next night. The contrast now would have been too painful!

14

Chilly & unsettled. Heard from C.S.D. & had a delightful letter from dear Screw. Bless him! I can't go till Saturday, as I could not engage the Coupée of the Diligence to myself before. I wish I had known this: I could have heard from Screw after he had received the rem^r of the note & the cheque. Dined again at *Les 3 frères*, which I like the best.

15

Finer, till it clouded over & grew dark & chilly about 4. I think every night of going to some theatre, but my courage always oozes out by the time dinner is over; & so it is with my visit to Versailles; I shall never accomplish it. Dined again at *Les 3 frères*; decidedly the best I have found. (Casimir)

No letter, so I shall have none till Venice. Same cold, uncertain weather. Dined as yesterday, Casimir, but I have lost all taste & pleasure. I hate Paris & the French. Wrote a last letter from Paris to Screw, inclosing him a Print.

Same uncertain Weather. Wrote to Antonio. Dined as yesterday.

Weather still uncertain. Dined early at *Les 3 frères*. Left the railway station at 10 minutes after 8. I had been waiting in the Diligence unnecessarily since $6\frac{1}{2}$. To Tonnerre by rail, then with Horses to Chalons, which we reached at $4\frac{1}{2}$. Ugly country, & air very chilly. The Coupée very uncomfortable, & would have been unbearable but I had taken the whole, & Quinlan was quiet & took little room. *Hotel du Parc* at Chalons where 16 or 17 years ago I was with Mrs. H^n and Miss Nepean. Mt. Blanc & the Jura ridge covered with Snow, very clear. But my thoughts turned to this day 3 weeks & poor Screw, & what will be his end, & to this day fortnight & my leave taking of Tom. Oh! my poor boy who is dead is the happiest. And then amid all this weakness comes the thought of dear Lady Q. & all her trials. What a world of woe it is, & who would wish to stay in it!

Fine, that is a hot sun & bitter cold wind. Off by steam boat a little after 8 & got into the 'Hotel de l'Univers' at Lyons at $3\frac{1}{2}$. I am weary & unwell in mind & body, but the former suffers the most. A fortnight today I left London: 3 weeks today I saw Screw for the last time, & he deceived me: – 45 weeks since I first spoke to Jack: – 40 since we went to Gravesend! the last time I was in a steamer on a river was with him. So passes time; such are the pleasures of memory! As we approached Lyons the banks of the river were pretty; before, all was very tame. They did not open anything on disembarking. I start to-morrow at $3\frac{1}{2}$ a.m. & hope to reach Marseilles to sleep. I have no quiet till I reach Venice & my letters, if Screw is not faithless; but I doubt of all & everything.

21

Same weather. Got up to be on board at $3\frac{1}{2}$ & we did not make a start till $5\frac{1}{2}$, having got one of the wheels entangled in some rope. A filthy boat, & the voyage most fatiguing & the Rhone less fine than I had fancied, or I daresay the reason was that I am come to the '*nil admirari*'. I thought more of our excursion from Gravesend to Sheerness 40 weeks ago than of the *pittoresque* of the Rhone. Got to Avignon very tired about 5. Dined & went to bed, having picked up a bad cold, if nothing else. Gen¹ Fox came from Lyons by the boat.

22

Madᵉ Pierron's Inn clean & comfortable. Got off by rail at $6\frac{1}{2}$ & reached Marseilles before 11. Some pretty scenery about *L'Etang de Berre*, & saw Arles & Tarascon. Made some acquaintance with Gen¹ Fox.

Inn here good – 'Hotel d'Orient'. Does not stink as that of Beauvau did: but I think the harbour is less offensive than formerly. Morning fine, but about midday it became cold & showery. Wrote & sent letter to Screw. And now my damned luck has played me a pretty trick. There is a Quarantine put on at Genoa for all *provenienze* by sea from Marseilles, & it is supposed the same will be done at Leghorn. Some ship from Rio lost 3 men with yellow fever, & the authorities here admitted her to free *pratique*, & so the Genoese have put Marseilles in Quarantine! A nice fix! I cannot get the Coupée of the Diligence to Nice (even supposing the land communication is left open) till Sunday: so I have sent off Quinlan to see if he can hire me a carriage for a reasonable Sum, & then I will post it to Nice, & get off tomorrow afternoon. Oh! Screw! if it had not been that I delayed my departure a week in the hope (a false one as it turned out) of seeing more of you, I should have escaped all this confusion! I am the most unlucky rascal, & now the expense of my Journey will be doubled at least. But I am so weary & so eager to be at Venice that I will run any extra expense to get there – perhaps to be still more disappointed!

23

Tolerable day. Saw the consul, Mr. Turnbull, the Quarantine is confirmed at Genoa & there is no doubt of the same at Leghorn. I have decided on waiting here for the Coupée of the Diligence to Nice on Sunday – a most annoying delay, but better than 6 days quarantine, & they demand so exorbitantly for the hire of a carriage to Nice that, with the expense of posting, it would be ruinous. Genl Fox seems to have resolved to make the quarantine & go tomorrow morning by the Steamer. He would, I think, have been easily persuaded to club with me in posting, but He objects to *forced marches* by night. (He is going to meet his wife, & I to find letters); & I do not feel companionably disposed. Curious! but I am to be charged with Despatches for Mr. Abercrombie, if I go by Turin! I would gladly have declined, but knew not how to get out of it without a greater mess than I am in already!

Uncertain – 37 weeks today since dear Jack was buried. Oh! how weary is this existence, how dreadful is all this delay! I can neither read, nor write, nor find Interest in anything. What shall I become when settled again at Venice? I can hope for nothing better than to fall into a monotonous state of Vegetation, & must be content if I can only maintain quiet & order in my Household. I can no longer struggle, or find fault, & feel that I shall become a slave: but what is there now worth contesting about! Yet if I could muster resolution to use my reason, I might know that to this, or to worse, it must have come, sooner or later, even had my poor Boy lived, & that the rest is the natural consequence of what has been done before. I wish that I had not fallen in with Gen¹ Fox: it will lead to some embarrassment when He comes to Venice, for He is recommended to Mr. Browne, & He has himself proposed to call upon me there. What could I say or do in this, or in the case of the Despatches! I leave all to chance.

Screw! I long for your letters: they amuse me. If I am disappointed (as I must own I probably shall be) then I shut out all future day dreams, & must only mourn for the dead, & still more deeply for the living. Poor dear Lady Q!

24

First day of Summer. Took Physic last night, thus turning my untoward delay to some account. Mr. Turnbull having given me an admission to the '*cercle*', I go there for the papers, & find it a great resource. Genl Fox went at 4 P.M. He is to do four days quarantine on board at Genoa, & then the Vessel will be admitted to free *pratique* at Leghorn. There are said to be many Passengers, so I prefer my own decision, though I would rather have avoided Turin. I have secured the Coupée to myself. The Genl is agreeable, & seems to be what I have always heard of him, very amiable. Had I encouraged it, I think He would have gone with me to Nice, & so on by land; but I said nothing more than that he was '*Padrone*'. I wish we had not met. Wrote to Elizabeth Sabine.

25

Very fine. A flower show in the *cortile* of the Hotel: Roses, verbenas, & especially Antirrhinums very good. Read *Galignani* of 22nd – Wednesday. Tomorrow I set off once more, on my tedious journey! Would it were over, & then there remains but that other one, for which I long most earnestly. I must make a new Will as soon as I am settled. I know not why, but I am even unusually depressed today, & feel a presentiment of something wrong coming! To drown thinking I went & called on Mr. Turnbull, & sat for some time, but nothing will do. Among the roses are some very pretty new varieties of variegated, very delicate. A White Rhododendron, new to me, labelled '*Noblenorum*', which is Hebrew to me. I almost regret that I did not break up my Establish-

ment at Venice, sell my chattels, & remain in England!
But then, as things are, *cui bono*? and there were so
many objections. I wish I had not met G^l Fox: it
annoys me in so many ways. Yet I don't see that I
could have done more than I did; for I certainly made
no advances towards his acquaintance, & at Avignon
kept out of his way, till we were thrust into the same
carriage: then we came to the same Hotels, a thing
perfectly accidental, for I let Quinlan select for me,
& He did well in his choice, I must allow. The Hotel
here, 'D'Orient', is really excellent, & the people very
civil.

26

Sunday. Fine weather seems to be set in & I shall
have a hot journey to what I feel is my last Home.
Coupée small & narrow: quite insufferable if we were
3 in number. Got off a little after 6 a.m. [*Heavily
erased:* 'This day 3 weeks Tom Roberts & Blues; to
the grave of my poor Jack for the last time. This day
4 weeks Screw at the Gds the last time. What will
become of him? He got his discharge on Tuesday the
30th April. I heard of it on the 2nd May.']

27

Got to Nice about 10 a.m. A fatiguing journey, but
weather favourable, cloudy, not very dusty & not too
hot. But nothing, not even my own blue Med^n, has
charms for me now. 'Hotel des Etrangers'. Consigned
Despatches to M. La Croix, jun^r, the Consul.
[*Passage very heavily erased:* This day 4 weeks saw
Screw for the last time. 46 weeks since I spoke last to
poor Jack. Of such recollections is my life now made

up.] Twice I have been here before, in 33 & 36. How different now! As some relief I can go on to Genoa tonight in the *Dante*, & thus escape Turin: but, oh! the weariness of this mode of travelling!

28

We got off last night at 6 (At the same hour, 46 weeks ago, I took leave of J.B. on the 9th July to go to Coolhurst) & reached Genoa at 6½, & I was through all forms & Custom Houses & in the Hotel about 8, but the boat is a slow one.

'Hotel des 4 Nations'. No place by the courier either tonight or tomorrow, so I must put up with a slow Diligence in which I have secured the Coupée. A month since Screw quitted the Blues. Poor fellow! I fear he will repent. Set off about 8 P.M. At Novi transferred to a rail road – at Alessandria Diligence again. Ticino immensely swelled, & passengers & baggage all trundled into one very small boat: passage difficult & dangerous. Got to Milan past 9 P.M. of the 29th, the most fatiguing & worst journey I ever performed. Dead tired with 3 nights without undressing. Bairr's at Milan. Weather favorable, but the country looked very bad, floods, & the Oaks & Planes stripped of their leaves. And now that I am here, within 24 hours of Venice, I almost dread to go on, for I fear not finding any letter, & then I should be almost mad. I know all my folly, but there seems a fate that drives me on, & which I cannot struggle against. I left the Hotel at Nice at the same time as that on which I first took leave of J.B. on 9th July, 46 weeks ago. After dinner at Genoa I felt so overcome, that if my spirits sink thus it must be over soon. I was & am half out of my mind, without any particular reason for the increase of dejection, except the anxiety about a letter & the dread of being disappointed, as I have a sad presentiment will be the case. Venice is my cry, though I am nearly beat by fatigue. There I shall find a letter, or know the worst. Oh! Screw, Screw! or rather Jack! Jack! for it is the recollection of you that haunts me. I feel as if I were running after some great misfortune, urged on by an irresistible power. Tonight I feel certain that I shall find no letter, & then I know not what the effect will be on my nerves.

30

A tolerable night's rest. Called on the Millards. Engaged Place for the courier who starts tomorrow at 5 P.M. & gets to Venice at 3 P.M. on Saturday. Packed up presents for Screw. *Fête Dieu*, but I did not go to see the procession. A bore, for no business is done. Ld Northampton, &c., arrive here on Saturday, having reached Genoa yesterday, so I just missed them all.

31

Cloudy, but good for travelling. At last then the day is come for finishing my travels, & tomorrow I shall be at Venice & know my fate! I tremble & doubt, & know not how I shall bear my solitary life contrasted with English recollections. But one is dead, the other no longer a gallant Blue, & what should I have found to replace two such rare fellows! All I hope for & request is quiet, if my domestics will let me have it. On reaching Milan on Wednesday night it was exactly 41 weeks since I left Jack to go to Scotland! and now – death & madness!

Never let any one make the journey from Genoa to Milan as I did. The luggage was discharged & loaded again seven or eight times before reaching Milan, & if the weather had been bad I know not what must have happened. Custom Houses everywhere most civil & obliging. Passports tiresome; but no wonder after the last two years. Got off from Milan about 6½ P.M. Stopped at Brescia, & was forced to get out while they took out the Bags. Then had to wait two Hours at Verona for the train: then slowly to S. Giuliano, where we got into boats, & I was almost broiled with the Sun. Finally got into my own House about 4 P.M. on Saturday the 1st of June, after an absence of a year within a few days. Antonio was gone to look for me, but Teresa told me there *was* a letter, & when He came back He gave me such a one from Screw, as made me feel better than I have done for some weeks. It was all I could wish, & much more than I expected. Bless him for it.

My Apartment looks nicer & cleaner than anything I have seen for a long time, & all appears *couleur de Rose*, & I am so satisfied with my letter that I see, too, all *en beau*. May it last!

June 2

Cloudy, but fine & hot. I think I felt so for the first time since I left S. Lazzaro last year. I never moved, but occupied myself with beginning to re-arrange things, & in writing to Screw & thanking him for his. This day month I visited poor Jack's grave. Shall I ever see it again?

3

Weather uncertain, but I went out in the boat to Mr.

Mudie's & Lady Sorell's. I never saw anything so mournful as this first aspect of Venice. It has the air of being deserted & abandoned to the Elements. The depression & despair are said to be general. Occupied myself with the disagreeable, but necessary, task of destroying old letters. How many recollections of the past, as I looked through Craven's, Lady Coventry's, Lady Queensberry's, &c!

4

Weather is warm, but unsettled. Wrote to Lady Q. & to Marino Torlonia. Went to see my good friends at S. Lazzaro, but Padre Gregorio was absent, & had been so a long time; the Archb^p was expected hourly from Padua. Padre Pasquale in Villeggiatura, & the Padre to whom I had promised the flower seeds was in Asia Minor: thus all were dispersed, & I saw only P. Raffaelle, who received me kindly. I left the flower seeds & a snuff Box for the Archb^p, & came away. In the Evening I walked out for the first time, & went to the Piazza; I never saw such an abandoned look: not a face I knew, & nothing but the lowest class, & a few German Officers: not even any appearance of Police, Gendarmerie, or military: – a desert, & the Port empty. Let the lovers of Revolution, or Reform as Ld Palmerston calls it, come & see what Italy is. The air is hot & stifling tonight. I hardly see how one will be able to continue here; even careless about society as I am!

5

Cloudy & showery. Wrote to Mrs. H. & to Screw, with the rem^r of the note. This day nine months my best Jack died, & with him half my heart. Poor dear

Boy! He sleeps, I trust, well; nothing can grieve him more!

Settled my accounts and began afresh after a very expensive year. I have squandered a good deal, but for my best Jack, & for Screw. I feel no regret at what was given to them. Now I must economize, & truly here I see no reason or inducement to spend anything extra. So I shall be able to send a tip to Screw, sometimes, to encourage him in his virtuous ways. A month since I left England! Very warm, the first real warmth I have felt for a year!

I find no one here: it is the City of the Plague and it almost overcomes me. I do not know how I shall support such total solitude. What a contrast to life in London, the roystering Blues, and all! But Jack is gone, & Screw left! and after them there was nothing to attach oneself to, tho' there were some fine, saucy blackguards still. Here I am absolutely alone. If my spirits will bear it, so much the better.

6

Warm & pleasant. By degrees I am finding out my ways & things: but I have no heart to set about putting Books &c. in order, or in dressing out my rooms. I really feel that I care for nothing, save a letter from Screw, poor fellow! About the 26th, as I calculate, I may hope to hear that He has received all that I have sent him.

The motto on the Sun dial at St. Feriol (where the great reservoir of the Languedoc canal is) is '*Sol me, vos umbra, regit.*'

I have been reading over, in order to destroy, old pocket books & journals. Alas! what scenes of other days they called up!

Beastie died on the 17th Septr 1827.

On Tuesday the 15th April 1828, Sontag made her Debut, C.S.D. & self in Mrs. T. Dickins' box.

In June (the 4th) 1829, went with Bailey to the Derby – on the 29th with him to the Nore. He seems to have gone away in September, but I find a mem: so erased that I cannot make it out, '13 Nov^r, last time in the morning' – the rest illegible; but I suppose having reference to him. Afterwards, on the 9th July 1831, I find 'Abschied' marked, which I think must refer to the same person.

Continuing these sad reminiscences I find on the 16 June 1835 that I heard of the fate of the poor fellow, but it is not noted what that fate was, or from whom I heard it. My own recollection tells me it was from one of his comrades, & that He had deserted & entered the Portuguese service, where, it was supposed, he had died! I think the person who told me must have been *Gilpin*.

This is fifteen years ago! What things to look back on! And now I am old indeed – older in mind, too, than in body! Would it were all over, for my weariness grows insupportable, & I can scarce struggle on from day to day. Thank God! I have had the resolution to go through & destroy a long series of letters, notes & recollections. The effort has been painful, & now that they are perished, & with them much forgotten, I feel relieved, & yet the act has left upon my mind a sadness & depression which oppress me grievously. The next thing to be done is the same with my journals, & yet I go on keeping this!

7

Fine & warm. I long for another letter; though I own

it is most unreasonable to expect one yet for some time; if it had not been that Screw talked of writing again in a week. He will do so when He has received his things by Shea & got my letters from here. I will be patient, & try to be reasonable. I think C.S.D. grows cold and less frequent in his correspondence.

8

Fine. This day year (but after midnight) I went on board the *Racer*! Little did I think what sorrow awaited me! Eleven months today I first saw Jack! I never can forget the Impression He made on me, though we did not speak. Poor boy! How I envy you your cold grave! But cut off so suddenly, so young, so beautiful! Oh! Jack! and none to remember you but myself! Got a thundering letter from Screw, full of kindness. It had been lying for four days at the P.O. here, from their carelessness. A little rain at night.

9

This day year at 3 a.m. I went on board the *Racer*. Wet & rather cooler.

10

Fine, but looking rather unsettled. Wrote to Screw, &, after I had posted it, got another stunner from the rare boy.

11

Fine. Began to dine early & then to Lido. Sent a letter to C.S.D.

12

Same. I calculate that today Screw will have received both my letters from Venice & that from Milan, & have got his parcel. How I should like to be by when he opens the roll. In the evening I went to the Armenians, but my friend P. Gregorio is absent &, as I suspect, under some cloud – q. Mad^e Gabriel? The Archb^p out of spirits & all I talked to very desponding & dissatisfied.

13

Cloudy but warm. No letter from C.S.D. – no answer from Marino – I am rather anxious about the latter, for I think some family misfortune must have fallen on him. Nothing now surprises me. Evening showery.

14

Weather unsettled. Still no letters from C.S.D. or from Marino. Wrote to Screw & sent him my Dream. Heard again from Screw, but after I had sent mine. He had not heard from me yet.

15

Same unsettled looking weather. I long so for my next letter, for then, I hope, He must have received the things by Shea, & I'm sure the Pictures will make him as happy as can be, & that he will write me a stunner in return. Went to the Lido after dinner.

16

Fine. My damned cook plagues me, & I fear won't answer, but I will try & be satisfied.

17

Fine. No letters again today. I do hope that tomorrow will bring me one from Screw, tho' I am not sure till Thursday, I fear: if I do not hear then my first must have been stopped. To Lido in the evening. The Venetians are as mad & foolish as ever, in their talk at least.

18

Heard that the Ship with my goods was arrived. I believe I should have been better pleased she had been lost, & I had had my £200 Insurance, for I have little use for the things here. Thundery all day. No letters, & I believe I could not have had one for the last date from Paris is the 11th – & Screw could not have written till that day: but I am so eager to have his next that every hour seems a day, till it comes. Very heavy rain about midday.

St. David's day is the 30th December. Mem: to send Screw £5 for it.

Went to Lido & got home just as the rain came on.

19

Stormy night & wet day. A letter from M. Torlonia but none from Screw. If none comes tomorrow I shall be very uneasy about my things by Shea & my letters from hence. All kinds of difficulties about my things from England. The Ship is arrived, but they say that almost all the articles are not to be admitted at any duty, & even my old clothes are refused. So there must be Petitions & God knows what ceremonies & expense, & after all I shall not get out half, I suppose. Wrote to Screw, having lost my patience, not with Him, but with the delay which I apprehend, if not loss of things & letters. If he posted a letter on the 12th, it ought to be here, and he should have got my first on the 10th at latest. Heigh Ho! What a fool I am! Yet I am really very fidgetty & long to hear from the Boy. Got a letter from M. Torlonia, so that it does not seem there is any neglect in the delivery here. Patience till tomorrow!

20

Cloudy & chilly: the weather seems to have broken & to be nearly what it was last year at this time. This day last year I left Vienna. How little I dreamed of what I was so soon to find, & too soon to lose for ever, in England. I am very low today; partly, I suppose, the effect of the weather, & partly from being so anxious till I hear once more from Screw. As to my Custom House difficulties here, they serve to talk about, but I really care little about the result! Give me a letter today, & I shall be better again. I am less uneasy, because He has been so good in writing four times, without having heard from me. Poor Boy! I should like to see him when he receives mine sent yesterday! Poor boy! my dear Jack is the best off: nothing more can harm or disturb him. Would I were with him! Screw already feels that the happiest days of his life were those passed among the gallant Blues, when Jack was his Pal. Could I but have known those Boys together! & had Jack lived I must have done so soon. And then – what would have become of me, for I should have been capable of committing any extravagance for them! No letter, which makes me very uncomfortable. I cannot at all understand it for there might have been one up to the

13th inclusive, which allows 3 days after mine of the 2nd must have reached him, if it ever reaches at all. This expectation wears me out. Perhaps the Ascot Races may have prevented his writing. It rained incessantly all day & was very cold. A longer day I have seldom toiled through. Now I do not expect to hear before Monday. If not then, I shall write, for I shall suspect that *prepaying* here is not safe.

21

Same weather, & I have returned to winter trousers, & could bear a fire well. Will today produce anything? I try to think that I shall not be disappointed, & that I do not expect now till Monday: yet secretly I do hope for a letter today: how I long for it I can't say. And yet it is reasonable that I should wish to know that a letter post paid arrives safe, of which, as yet, I have no certainty. *Voilà*! here is my justification! No letter, & I now begin to fear seriously that none of mine have ever reached him. Screw, I will wait over Monday, & then, if I do not hear something, I will send a single letter on Tuesday not paid, for I can bear the suspense no longer. If I only knew that one had reached him, I should feel easy, but till I know that I am in alarm lest they have pocketed the Postage money & destroyed the letters. After a very wet morning the weather cleared, but it is chilly & unsettled.

22

Still chilly & looking doubtful. I wonder whether I shall have better luck today. I will wait over Monday night's Post, & then, if I get none, will post mine on Tuesday without prepaying. He had been so quick in writing his two last, that he has spoiled me. '*L'appétit vient en mangeant*', & as there was money I want to ascertain whether it is safe to send it so. It answered from Paris. He is such a wild fellow that I still hope he has been out larking & that is the reason I don't hear. However, Patience till Tuesday.

Three weeks today since I got here. They seem like 3 years – an eternity – I feel myself as in a dream – nothing is real about me – nothing save the misfortunes! – Poor Jack – poor Lady Q! What an association of names! Good God! surely I am mad – madder than many who are shut up! No letter; so that now I am quite at a loss to account for this so unexpected silence, except by supposing that none of mine, i.e. neither of the 2nd or 5th, or the things by Shea, have been delivered: & the failure of the last is even more puzzling to me than that of the letters. However, I will wait the result of tomorrow & Monday's courier, & then write without paying the postage. And if the poor Boy should be ill. Poor dear Jack! your fate is always before me! The weather is wretched.

My goods are all locked up in the Dogana, & I get no answer to my Petition, nor hear anything of the liberation of those that have only the duty to pay; – yet all this would have no effect upon me, if I could but have a line from Screw. I cannot help fearing that all my letters have been stopped for the sake of embezzling the Postage, & that, very naturally, he will not write again, thinking that I have deserted him. But then the things which Shea was to carry over! &, as I understood, He was to be in London by the 10th. In short, I am more disheartened & sad about all this of poor Screw than I can venture to admit, even to myself: & now I really despair of hearing at all, unless the letter which I will post on the 25th reaches him, & for that I must find [wait?] till the middle of July!!! Would I had laid my bones by my dearest Jack's!

23

Another wet day: as yet nothing like summer, & the longest day is gone. Alas! all are long alike to me. I can only explain this silence by my letters having been stopped here, to embezzle the Postage. This would account for them; but then how to explain the things given in charge to Quinlan? In short, I am puzzled, & another such week of suspense & expectation would wear me out & quite turn the little sense I have left to madness.

I have fidgetted on till it is 12 o'clock, & now I have the relief (& it is one) of thinking that in 48 hours more I shall post my letter, if in the interim I do not hear (& I have no hope of doing so), & then I think by the *fifth* of July I must know what it means: – something to look forward to my *Birthday* for! What an existence – & for how long must I endure it! Seven weeks today since I was at his grave – since I last saw the Blues: – eight since I last saw Screw in harness!

Got a glorious letter from Screw – all right. He had got his french things & liked them, & had been on a lark, as I suspected, down to Ascot. They opened my letter at 'Les Rousses' – so I suppose Mr. Shea enlightened his mind & morals by reading it – nice literature, & there was a note, too, for Tom Roberts in it!!

24

Wrote to Screw & sent him another £5 for a lark on
my birthday – his is 16th Decr. He is 26!!! Weather
mending, but still not settled. Now I have only got
to deliver my goods from this damned Custom
House, & then my troubles appear over. But they
are so cursed slow about everything official! One
would think there was treason in a box of old
clothes, or some packets of Medicine! God help me
through it this time, & I will never venture anything
again by Sea. I might have brought it all in by land
without trouble, or even examination.

25

Fine. Tried dining early again. It is an existence, this,
& there is no life in it – nothing like the rollicking,
blaggard Blues: but I am really comfortable, well
lodged, and the Household, apparently, content &
wishing to remain so. Society there is absolutely
none, &, but for the newspaper, I might as well be in
one of the far Isles of the Pacific: but though a little
society would be sometimes agreeable, I am not sure
that I am not better thus, for I hate the restraint of
being expected to be agreeable, & there is so *very*
little society that amuses or interests me: as for the
crowd it bores me to extinction. And so, except a
letter from Screw, I have nothing to look for to
break the dull monotony of Day by Day! In the
evening to the Lido.

26

Summer seems to be come at last – the hot weather
which poor Jack complained of last July. Seasons are

without change for him now! They send me word that orders will be issued in a day or two for my things to be passed. One more trouble over! No letters from England. I cannot understand why C.S.D. does not write. Mrs. H. will hardly answer mine, & Lady Q. – alas! what can she write about? The Peers of England have condemned Lord Palmerston by a majority of 37. Will he resign after such an affront as no other Foreign Minister, in England, ever received? After dinner to the Lido.

27

Fine. This day year I left Berlin! At night a storm, so that I could not go to the Lido.

28

Hot & languid. The Minister of finance is here, so I must wait till next week – & how much longer! – for my poor things. The weather was so uncertain again tonight that I did not go to the Lido.

29

Scirocco. I have been here a month today. It seems an Eternity & yet, all things considered, it has gone by with fewer *dispiaceri* than I might have expected. Screw has been good hitherto, & has written five times. The days pass by somehow, & if I have no pleasure, I am, at least, quiet. One should ask for no more after 60. Why should one live after fifty? C.S.D. does not write – Why? I hope for another from Screw tomorrow or next day. In the Evening to the Lido.

30

Fine & hot. As the day approaches on which, last year, I reached England, I feel my spirits sadden & my heart sink. Tomorrow, & the year will have passed away, & with it how much sorrow has come upon me, & how bitter are the recollections that now every day will recall poor Jack, so soon cut off! Yet how happy his fate to dear Lady Q's or my own! I feel very, very low today, as if I should have no letter; indeed with this new alteration of the P.O. in London in compliance with the whims of the Saints, I suppose I can have none till tomorrow. What a state they are in between the Saints & their fanaticism, & Lord Palmerston & his insolent meddlings! A pretty figure the H. of C. will cut when it sends an Address to the Queen, praying to go back to the former conduct of the P.O.: – & what an honorable one the F.O. cuts in the sight of Europe with the concession to France, & the tone which the French take in condescending to be pacified! Verily Lord P. is the curse of the civilized World! & to be content to be shielded & protected by Mr. Roebuck!!!

No letters! I am such a fool that, though I have had five letters from him here, & that probably He is waiting to send me something, I am quite dispirited at not hearing today. Now, most likely, I shall not till the end of the week. This is madness – I know it – & what will it be? Would I were in the grave with poor Jack!

July 1

A very overpowering hot night, & I suffering in mind & body. This day year I landed in England, & was at this time in London. Oh! the gallant Blues!

Oh! the days that are passed! And now how weary I am, & how weary are the present, how miserable those to come!

The cursed Customs House keeps all my things, those even which pay a fixed duty, & I have no means of guessing even when the day of their delivery will come. In the meantime I am much in want of some of them, & some are spoiling. This all arises from Mr. Mudie's stupidity. *Pazienza*! Today I do not expect any letter, probably shall have none before Saturday or Sunday. The cursed Methodists have made one lose one if not two days.

After all the fault was in the Post here. There were two letters from Screw, one came the 28th & the other yesterday, & one from C.S.D. Screw's stunning; but the poor fellow wants me to do more than I can, & I am afraid He will get into trouble – consequently that I shall be in a scrape – It would serve me right for my Imprudence – madness, rather – & will be entirely my own fault; for I could not reproach him, whatever may happen. He had left me & I was gone so that He never could have heard of me again. However there is not a word in his letters that can be construed wrong & I have confidence in him, for He has shewn himself uniformly an honest, honorable fellow: but He is wild as the winds (or I should not have taken so to him) – & he will take some business, neglect it, & fail. To Lido at night, i.e. after dinner.

2

Great storm this morning, but cleared after breakfast. Wrote to Screw, telling him what I could, & would, do to help him. His answer will be a nervous one for me! poor fellow! Could not go to the Lido because one Gondolier chose to be beastly drunk, so I called on Lady Sorell.

3

Doubtful, but air pleasant. They say that some of my *notions* are to be released today, &, more extraordinary, a portion is come! Heard from Mrs. H. & kinder than usual. Mine had been cold enough! They have detained the bit of stuff to line my Cloak, & the braid for the Gondoliers' trousers, & some of the livery buttons, the greater part were in a box & passed unobserved; & they have kept my jar of Maldon Salt, which I cared more about than almost anything: but salt is a privation, & it is in vain to say that I want it as Medicine. So now I must have recourse to another way of getting it out. It seems there is a company (of honest men) who, as formerly, if not now, in England, undertake to get any thing out at so much per cent: & I have commissioned them to get me out my Notions, especially my Salt, for I can't eat the dirty stuff here, if I can help it.

4

Very hot, & I could not sleep, &, as is always the case with me, the sight of things which I was used to see in other places, and at other times, makes me low & melancholy. Heigh Ho! I wish, oh! how I wish it was over: 'after life's fitful fever he sleeps well.' Heard again from Screw; & such a letter!!! After dinner to the Lido. My things came well; nothing damaged, & only one bottle of boot varnish broken.

5

Fine. Another birthday! As I have said to so many, would it were the last! but I see, & I feel, no hope, for my Health continues good, tho' the melancholy of feeling encreases & renders me weary of everything. Wrote to Screw. He is telling me lies, poor boy, & I have a conviction that the money is to carry him to America – perhaps California – to die. And such will be the end of my knowledge of the Blues! I do not regret the money. Of what use is it to me; & if it can be of any to him, it is well spent. But I feel I shall never see him or hear of him again; & then I have no one with whom to speak of my poor Jack. So be it! I am benumbed & steeled to everything. Poor Screw! He will run headlong to ruin. I felt it would be so from the moment He left.

For my birthday recreations I have sent a letter to poor Screw, & have mourned over the view of poor Jack's cold grave. Oh God! were I but sharing it with him! In that grave, too, lies G. Wilcox, & I have the regimental canes of both, here in Venice! As I went out to get my Certificates signed (which I could not do for the Consul General is expected tonight or tomorrow & Mr. Mudie's deputyship is therefore suspended) I called on Mrs. O'Conor & on C^ss Balbi, & then came weary home. Ten months today since my dear Boy died – died while I was waiting, & chiding his delay! Before my next birthday (for, alas! I feel that there are others to be endured) I shall have to note down the loss of Screw – not by death, but by his going to America, on some wild scheme. All that I love is smitten with ruin!! *'Je porte malheur.'* The tints of the sky at Sunset tonight were the most beautiful I ever saw: azure & green & gold –

just such as Byron describes an evening on the
Brenta: – gorgeously beautiful to one who is in the
tune for admiring.

6

The night dreadfully hot: & I cannot sleep, & my
eyes begin to suffer from these long watchings. What
should I become without my sight?

7

Fifty two weeks today since in the Evening I first
saw John Brand! poor Boy! I trust you sleep in
peace, & wish I were by your side. Cloudy, but a
sharp scirocco, & I have a very bad cough which
shakes me terribly, but will do no more. I cannot get
my certificates, & must see about doing something
tomorrow, for should I die there are above £200 lost.
I am very low & out of spirits today. Poor dear
Jack! I shall not hear from Screw till next Sunday, I
think, & perhaps he may wait for my answer to his
of the 23rd.

Since I came here I have finished, with great per-
severance, Davila's *Guerre Civili* and now I am
straining my courage to undertake Guicciardini: for
I must do something, though nothing interests or
amuses me. Today I am totally '*désoeuvré*' and can
fix myself to nothing: my thoughts are of last year,
& my wishes for the grave. Who knows? – the very
malaise I suffer from today may be the prelude. One
day more & the *Anniversary* is come.

I did not leave the House, for in the Evening there
was a great deal of thunder & lightening, & I ached
from head to foot. Possibly the atmosphere so
charged with Electric matter may affect me: I know

not, but I never suffered so much from Heat & oppression. The storm seems to increase them instead of cooling the air. Alas! dear Jack! Nine weeks since I visited your grave!

8

Stormy & doubtful & Scirocco, very overpowering. I am completely knocked down. This day year what a beautiful apparition! how soon to disappear for ever! So young, so beautiful, so gay! & yet there was a melancholy in those large soft eyes, & about the smile of those lips, which seemed to say they were not long for this world. Poor Jack! a few weeks – a few days, I may say – & you passed away from me for ever! But your memory will never leave me, Boy! for you I would even live over again the last sad year!

The Paper brings the news of the death of Sir R. Peel on Tuesday night, the 2nd. He is an immense loss to his Country in the present state of Politics. The D. of Wellington must fall soon in the course of nature, & then there is no safety drag left. Peel's death was caused by a fall from his Horse. How strange that none die a natural Death!

Evening chilly & gloomy, gloomy as my own feelings & recollections. Alas! my dear Jack!

9

Cloudy & unsettled & cooler. This day year, Dear Boy, about this hour, I saw you in all your beauty, smiling as your gallant charger reared & pranced, & then you recognized me. It was the only time I ever saw you in full uniform. And then in the Box I spoke to you, & after Parade we met for five minutes, & you told me your name. I see the spot, I see you now,

Jack, & my spirit is dead within me, for you are gone, & there is nothing like you left.

The last present I made Jack – the last I made Screw – was a knife: – the last thing I received from each was a reg¹ button. I have a feeling that I shall write once more to Screw, i.e. with his money, & that then I shall never hear more of him. Time will shew whether I have too bad an opinion of human nature. I try to think otherwise, but my misgiving is this: & why should I wonder if it is accomplished? Reason tells me it is only the natural consequence.

Ten minutes after 4 P.M. At this moment last year I was talking to you, Jack, & you were telling me your name: just opposite the passage up to New Street, & under a large tree. I see you now, Boy! Would that you could see me! or that I were in your grave & you yet living! Yet why? Surely, surely, you are the one to be envied: your cares are over, & probably life had little bright in store for you. And yet you were contented! So young, so good, so beautiful! If there be another life, Jack, oh! may you be happy!

Today, too, Screw will have got my answer. Will he be satisfied? I must think well of the bold boy, and that He will be grateful. It was just possible that I might hear from him today, & though I had no right to expect to do so, I could not help asking anxiously if there was any letter for me. There was none, & it was only *just possible* there should be. I ought not to expect one before Sunday. A wet night.

10

In the night, or rather about $2\frac{1}{2}$ a.m. this morning, a smart shock of Earthquake, which shook my light

Iron bedstead. The other floor of this House being uninhabited, the Rats have taken possession & make a dreadful clatter all night, & I am afraid of using poison for fear of the stench if they die. It is a great nuisance though, for their noise is insufferable. Weather stormy & quite unsettled, so that there is no going to Lido of an Evening: & so I dine late, yet still there is a long light interval before candles, & I cannot sit down to read by that light, & I am restless & low, for each day recalls what I was doing, or *hoping*, last year.

Shall I hear from Screw today? No! – and yet I cannot but hope till the return from the Post dispels doubt. Ah me! A horrid wet day! I wrote to Screw – poor Boy! & sent him a note which he could shew his father to bear out the story which he says he told him about poor Jack's relation. No letter, except a Dun.

11

This day year I first wrote to my dear Jack! *Ned Harvey!* I think on Sunday I shall hear: but the carelessness of the P.O. here is scandalous. The letter I got yesterday had come on the 8th, & yet they had given the Paper regularly! It is very tiresome, as one can feel no security. The weather seems mending, but it is still chilly & unsettled, too much so to dine early.

12

Another shock of Earthquake about midnight. Today tolerably fine, but the air chilly. I now despair of a letter before Sunday. This day last year Jack received my first, & answered it directly. He was on guard at the

Hyde Park gate, & complained of the Heat, Poor boy!

In the afternoon it began again to thunder & lighten & rain, & my Head is sadly affected the last two days with this atmosphere. No letter. I suppose he waited to write after his lark on the 5th. If so, on Sunday I may hear: or, perhaps, he will wait to know my answer about his money, & then I shall not hear till Wednesday. I know that it is quite natural that he should wait to write till after the 5th, at any rate, for I had told him to give me an account of his flare up; but I am unwell & nervous this Evening, & have a pressentiment that something is wrong. Yet the last letter was as honest & proper as I could wish; still, I fear for him, & that some mischief is brewing for him. On Tuesday or Wednesday I must hear, for He will want his money whatever his plans may be. Poor Screw, I shall miss his letters so much, & he is the last link left of poor Jack.

13

This day year I got my first letter from poor Jack! I shall not hear from Screw till tomorrow, & I fear that, owing to his letter not having been delivered here till the 1st, I shall not hear till Wednesday; for He will have expected the answer on the 7th, & will think I am angry or shabby. Weather chilly & un-settled. No letter; if none comes tomorrow, I shall be very much disappointed; but must resign myself till Wednesday.

14

A fine day at last. If I do not hear today, it will be all owing to the damned Post here, & poor Screw will be very uneasy for two days. But the villain ought to have written on the 7th at any rate, to tell me about his lark. There's nothing like my own poor Boy! Ten weeks today I visited his Grave, & then saw the last of the Blues. No letter – which is very natural, for he would wait in daily expectation &, perhaps, did not know exactly what tone to take, but very shabby, & my own Boy would have written about the fifth without waiting for more. But then there is nothing like him left.

The more I reflect, the more I fear He is telling me false, & that the money is to go to America or California. What he says of his marriage, that 'she would not have him now', would agree with this idea. And so ends my romance of the gallant Blues! Poor Jack! poor Screw! It was very unlikely that I should ever see you again, Screw, yet I had a hope; & now, tonight, I am more disappointed, & have more forebodings than I care to allow. I shall hear on Wednesday, if not before, – write & send him the money, & never hear of or from him again. Such are my anticipations: it is but fair to say that I deserve it, should they prove true; & have no right to wonder, or to blame. And I must admit, too, that, except the deceiving me before he left the regiment, I have no reason to justify me in doubting him now. *Nous verrons – Pazienza* – I am grown a Philosopher, which means, I care for nobody.

15

Weather still looks unsettled, & has no feel of summer. Two more days of expectation! & I am such a fool as to be really quite uncomfortable, not to say unhappy, at being so long without hearing. How I long for Wednesday's post!

16

Fine. Today, if he writes by return of Post, I ought to hear. If I do not today, or tomorrow, I shall be in despair. I sent my answer on the 2nd. He should receive it the 9th, & this is 16th, which allows 7 days for each; but then in order to hear today He must have been at Home & have written the same day he received mine. One more day of anxiety & patience, therefore. I am so nervous with the expectation of the result of the Post that I can fix myself to nothing. Curse you, Screw, why did you not write on the 7th? A letter from dear Lady Q. – melancholy enough! Alas! for her & her prospects. None from Screw; at which I am now puzzled beyond measure. If I do not hear tomorrow, I must write to know what it means.

17

Very fine & like settled Summer. Another disappointment. No letter, & I am perfectly bewildered. I fear the poor fellow is ill or has got into some trouble: & yet then he would surely write to me. All my former letters have gone safe, so that I have no reason to doubt these two having done so. It keeps me terribly nervous about him. Alas! poor Jack! with you I lost all. Yet Screw has behaved as well as possible always, & this inexplicable silence now proves that he is honest. Still I fear that something has happened to him, & that I shall hear of him no more! I did not know, nor dream, how much I was attached to him till this. What can it mean? They say, 'No news is good' & that ill flies apace: but I cannot satisfy myself thus. It is so strange that He should not have written instantly to get his £200!!

Wrote to Screw, & posted it myself. A storm at night, which drove me home, & I lost my row.

18

Storm again this morning early. Hot & languid. I have now left off expecting, & 'bide the time', but these few days of hope deferred have worried me much. I must try & grow wiser. This day year I received my second letter from poor Jack, complaining of the heat. Dear boy! *quando ullum inveniam parem!*

Heard from Screw. A wild kind of letter, & I can't make out what he is going to do: but the blaggard writes just as he acts, & there is no harm in him yet: but he'll never settle down to be steady.

19

Wrote to Screw with his money. Fine, but a storm again in the night. Rain in the Evening.

20

Wet. I never remember such unsettled weather. It is also Scirocco & very languid, & I am plagued with my Cough, & very dumpish & downish, & daily become more weary & indifferent of all & to all. Nothing but the stillness & absence of noise & society could make me support this place & this manner of life. But one is free at least from the plagues & duties of acquaintance.

Last night was the *Vigilia* of the fête of *Il Redentore*, formerly the most brilliant of Venice: even in my time very gay. Now nothing – Ah! Lord Palmerston! such are the effects of the Policy which Mr. Roebuck has thrown his shield over!

21

Fine; but I am out of spirits, for I am Dyspeptic again, & that always affects me, & now with my cough the straining incommodes me in another way; a way which I begin to fear will cause me one day serious suffering; & though I should be well content to die, let it be without *long* suffering previously. I ask no more.

22

Fine & hot like real summer. I do not think that I am quite right, yet I know not exactly where to put my finger on the sore. What a place this is become! the very throne of melancholy! Had a rare saucy letter from Screw. To the Lido after dinner.

23

Fine & pleasant. This day last year poor Jack wrote me his 3rd letter. Wrote a beastly one to Screw to go tomorrow. The blackguard has told me a hoax about his Garden, I suspect, & will be off on some wild scheme with his money. Never mind if he can enjoy it. I can't. After dinner to Lido.

24

Fine. Wrote to Screw.

25

Wet night & today showery. This was my poor Sister's birthday. She, at least, is happy, for She was without Sin. Her life prolonged would have been one of suffering, which she was mercifully spared. I envy her!

The Scirocco makes me feel low, & this way of life is not very exhilarating. *Pazienza*, there is an end to all, sooner or later! At night I was met at the Lido by the O'Conors, who insisted on my supping with them & some friends *en Gondole*. So I consented, & we supped by the light of the moon on the Laguna. It was brilliant moonlight, at the full, & calm & clear & beautiful & we had Ice & Champagne, &c. & there were Nicoletto Michiel & young Dolfin, &c. & it was really agreeable; but my thoughts wandered far away, & I was glad when it was over. I got home at 11 P.M. & found my Domestics wondering what had happened to their punctual old master.

26

Fine. This day last year poor Jack wrote me the last to Horsham, that He would meet me on the Evening of the 30th, but did not want anything; if He did he would tell me when we met! Poor boy! So soon to be cut off! Who remembers you now, Jack, save poor old Ned Harvey! May he soon follow you! The papers mention that the cholera has shewn itself again in London. I am very low today, & feel that I have courage neither to read or write. I suppose my last night's exertion was too much for my quiet habits.

27

Showery. Wrote to C. Dickins, to go tomorrow.
  In the evening to Lido.

28

Fine. Last year I was counting the Hours for the first evening with poor Jack on the 30th! Wrote to

Craven to Naples, to go tomorrow. My spirits are down at zero; & I can find no reason, save in my recollections & regrets for last year. 12 weeks today since I visited his grave, probably, for the last time. Who will ever do so now!

I have been thinking today that, probably, I shall hear once more from Screw: – I say *probably*, for it is very possible that, having got his money, he may be off, without my ever hearing more of him! I feel that He is thinking of America, or some Emigration, & it was for that view that he wanted money. If so, may He have good fortune in his undertaking! He will carry with him my best wishes. Then my *life* will be over; & a bare existence left. Poor Jack! bold Screw! you will be equally lost to old Ned. But one I shall envy – the other I envy not, even should California spare him & send him back loaded with Gold. Oh! the gallant Blues! oh, my beautiful Boy! oh, my brave Screw! What recollections!

29

Much rain early in the morning & showery afterwards. Last year on this day how I was calculating on the morrow's evening! Now what have I to hope for!

Yesterday's paper gave the account of the dinner to Ld Palmerston. Can degradation go further? The 3 Knights of the Bath, Naval, dirty Charley – Army, Sir de Lacy Evans of Spanish fame, - Civil, Himself! & praised for his courtesy by Mr. Bernal Osborne!!! None of his colleagues, a stray unknown Peer or two, & scarce a Gentleman, save his son Mr. Cowper or Temple. Poor Lady Palmerston! with a husband the Pet of the Radicals, the Helper's Helper of Ledru Rollin & Mazzini, the execration of every honest

Man throughout Europe! Shades of the Anti-Jacobin, of Sir A. Boswell, or of Theodore Hook, is there no one in these days to make a pendant to 'Michael's dinner'? First his Picture – next Mr. Roebuck's Vote of Approbation – then this dinner! Surely it is impossible to descend lower! How Princess Lieven must triumph in this disgrace, – for such even He must himself feel these *honors* to be. That in all the Army & Navy two such representatives could alone be found!

A thorough wet day. Recovered my Salt, which is an unspeakable satisfaction to me. I did not leave the House all day, & yet I want distraction, for each day now brings to my mind the saddest recollections of the last year.

30

Cloudy & wet & chilly. This day year I went to London from Coolhurst, & in the evening at the Arch at Hyde Park Corner met my poor Boy. We went together in a cab to Albany S^t, or one just by. It was then that, for the only time, I heard him sing. And then He laid his Head, with his beautiful Hair, on my shoulder. Poor, poor boy! Had you lived, Jack! what would have been your fate? I shall never see your like, & never forget you. Gentle boy! who & what were you? In the full hope & confidence that our Intercourse was only beginning, & that we should spend many months together, I merely marked down that we met. And now I try to recall every word, every action, every look, '*tam cari capitis.*' I did not then know how much I loved him, or how unlike He was to every one else. Peace be with you, Boy! & Mercy!

31

Weather cloudy & doubtful. A great ceremony (I did not go to it) on the Gesuits retaking possession of a part of their convent. I wrote to Marino Torlonia, it being his fête day. After tomorrow I shall wait anxiously for news from Screw. Shall I be disappointed? I know not, & am afraid to think how possible it is I may be so. Wrote likewise to Lady Q^y.

And now arrived at the end of July, I close this most melancholy Volume of my Diary. May I never finish another, for I am weary of life, & anxious for nothing but the grave where lies buried my dear Jack!

Appendix: The Diarist's Will

THIS IS THE LAST WILL AND TESTAMENT of me EDWARD LEEVES formerly of Tortington in the County of Sussex but now and for many years past residing in Venice   I give and bequeath unto my executors hereinafter named all my furniture of what kind soever plate wine linen china glass books pictures prints as well as all my private boxes with their contents together with whatever else I may die possessed of in my apartment in Venice to be by them sold and disposed of as they please but subject to the following bequests and payments videlicet   To each of my two women servants a year's wages   To Franz Schmiederitsch my man servant one hundred Napoleons in gold   To Giovanni Marassi one hundred and twenty Napoleons in gold and to my cook Jacques fifty Napoleons in gold, all to be paid without any deduction for legacy or other duties   If any or either of them should have left my service at the time of my decease my will is that her or his legacy to be held to be lapsed   I desire that all my clothes and wearing apparel be divided between the said Franz Schmiederitsch and Giovanni Marassi equally and with regard to any monies I may die possessed of in

England either in the three per cent Consols or being in the hands of my Bankers Herries Farquhar & Co or any sums which may be due or accruing to me at the time of my death I give and bequeath the whole amount thereof to my hereinafter named executors charging them to pay thereout one hundred pounds sterling free from all deductions to the Directors or Trustees of the British National Life Boat Institution and to Mrs. Charlotte Jefferies of Ebby Cottage near Stroud Water in the County of Gloucester the sum of fifty pounds sterling also free of all duty   Lastly I nominate and appoint my valued friends John S. Malcolm and Alexander Malcolm his brother of S. Benedetti [sic] in the City of Venice Esqrs. to be the EXECUTORS of this my Will and RESIDUARY LEGATEES subject only to the before mentioned legacies to the payment of any debts and to my funeral and testamentary expenses   I request the said Alexander Malcolm to accept and wear in recollection of me my gold repeating watch with the gold chain and anything attached thereto – EDWARD LEEVES – signed sealed published and declared as and for his last Will and Testament by the above-named Edward Leeves the testator in the presence of us who in his presence and at his request and in the presence of each other have hereunto subscribed our names as witnesses this ninth day of May 1870 – Sigismund Blumenthal – Alexander Blumenthal.

TRANSLATION FROM THE ITALIAN

Seen for a copy conformable with the original existing in this Royal Prefecture Venice the 30th August 1871.

Seal of the Prefecture
JOHN HARRIS
Sworn Interpreter to the Royal Provincial Tribunal.

I WILLIAM WEBB VENN of London Notary
Public by Royal Authority duly admitted and
sworn undersigned do hereby certify and attest unto
all whom it may concern that the foregoing writing
in the English language is a true and faithful Translation of the writing in the Italian language at the
foot of the document hereunto annexed under my
Official Seal and that full faith and credit may and
ought to be given to such Translation in the Courts
of Judicature and thereout – In testimony whereof I
have hereunto set my hand and affixed my said Seal
of Office to serve and avail where needful London
this second day of October one thousand eight
hundred and seventy one.

In fidem

WILLIAM W. VENN

Notary Public.

PROVED at London 30th Novr 1871 by the oath of
John Shiras Malcolm Esqre and Alexander Malcolm
(brother of the said John Shiras Malcolm) Esqr the
Executors to whom Adm[on] was granted limited
until the original Will or a more authentic Copy of
the said Will be brought into and left in the Principal
Registry of Her Majesty's Court of Probate.

Epilogue

Epilogue

POOR OLD LEEVES!
(Air: Three Blind Mice)

Poor old Leeves!
Poor old Leeves!
Was ever a man in so sorry a plight!
The Austrian forces are almost in sight,
So he's left for Trieste in the deuce of a fright –
      Poor old Leeves!

Soon Mayfair affords him the freedom to choose
Between elegant parties of dear Lady Q's
And the manlier charms of the rollicking Blues –
      Poor old Leeves!

He's often been warned so he cannot complain:
The landlord won't have it, he's told him again,
So he's out on the street in the wind and the rain –
      Poor old Leeves!

He's come down from Kinmount in the midsummer
   heat
And waited for hours at the end of the street,
But the dear boy is dead he was longing to meet –
      Poor old Leeves!

It is useless to mourn, as we all of us know,
But to Brompton each day grief compels him to go
And pour out his tears on a grave in the snow –
Poor old Leeves!

His spirits are low and his prospects are blue,
And by way of diversion he's nothing to do
But spend all his time and his money on Screw –
Poor old Leeves!

He's in Venice again, but he'll never forget,
And he's twenty years more to endure of it yet
With nought to console him, except mignonette –
Poor old Leeves!

John Sparrow